Isaac Newton wrote:

—On the sun and other heavenly bodies:

"This most beautiful system of the sun, planets, and comets, could only proceed from the counsel and dominion of an intelligent Being."

—On the Lord of the heavens:

"This Being governs all things, not as the soul of the world, but as Lord of all; . . ."

—On atheism:

"Atheism is so senseless. When I look at the solar system, I see the earth at the right distance from the sun to receive the proper amounts of heat and light. This did not happen by chance."

—On the solar system:

"The motions of the planets require a Divine Arm to impress them."

—On God, his Savior:

"The true God is a living, intelligent and powerful being."

—On the trials of life:

"Trials are medicines which our gracious and wise physician gives because we need them; and he proportions the frequency and weight of them to what the case requires. Let us trust his skill and thank him for his prescription."

—On God's presence:

"His (God's) duration reaches from eternity to eternity; His presence from infinity to infinity."

—On the Bible:

"I have a fundamental belief in the Bible as the Word of God, written by men who were inspired. I study the Bible daily."

ABOUT THE AUTHOR

John Hudson Tiner is a mathematician writing about a mathematician. Tiner's background as a scientist and faith as a Christian give him unusual insight into the religious life of Isaac Newton—the scientist and Bible scholar.

Tiner is the author of *When Science Fails* and has published in both secular and religious magazines, writing more than 200 articles dealing with science and religion. He has served as Editor of the *Journal of Arkansas Astronomical Association.*

He is an instructor of physics on the high school level and mathematics on the college level, and holds a Master's degree from Duke University.

INVENTOR, SCIENTIST, AND TEACHER

ISAAC NEWTON

John Hudson Tiner

ILLUSTRATED BY JONATHAN & DAVID INC.

MOTT
MEDIA
Milford, Michigan 48042

To John A. and Martha—My Parents

COPYRIGHT © 1975 by Mott Media, Inc.
Fourth Printing, 1988

Robert Burkett, Editor

LIBRARY OF CONGRESS CATALOGING IN PUBLICATION DATA

Tiner,John Hudson, 1944-
    Isaac Newton: The true story of his life.

    (The Sowers)
    Bibliography: p. 143
    Includes index.

    SUMMARY: A biography of the seventeenth-century English scientist who developed the theory of gravity, discovered the secrets of light and color, and formulated the system of calculus.
    1. Newton, Isaac, Sir, 1642-1727—Juvenile literature. [1. Newton, Isaac, Sir, 1642-1727. 2. Scientists] I. Jonathan & David, Inc. II. Title.

QC16.N7T56   509'.2'4 [B] [92]   75-32562
ISBN 0-915134-95-0 Paperbound

CONTENTS

CHAPTER ONE:

Christmas Baby

Between two and three in the morning of a cold
Christmas Day in 1642 two women rushed from
the Newton Manor in Woolsthorpe, England.
Their mission would take them to Lady Pakenham's mansion in North Waltham for a special
tonic. An infant had been born to Hannah Newton
that night. But he barely hung onto life.

A full moon guided them as they walked fast
over fields gleaming with frost. The younger
woman pulled her cloak closer and looked over
her shoulder. The English Civil War had begun.
Night raiders made local folks careful after dark.

The girl said, "Lady Pakenham's manor is only

a mile, but it seems much farther at a time like this." She shivered.

"Aye," the older woman said. "The infant is weak, barely able to cry."

Within thirty minutes the two women reached Lady Pakenham's manor and banged the household awake. A servant answered the door.

"We ask for a tonic for a gravely ill newborn infant," the older woman explained. "Hannah Newton's first child is a boy, but he is sickly and very small."

Lady Pakenham said, "It is Christmas night— and cold."

"Babies come on all nights, even cold ones," the older woman said.

Lady Pakenham said, "Come by the fire and warm. My servant will prepare the medicine you seek."

The older woman said, "I fear we will not find the infant alive upon our return." She sighed. "How can such a child accomplish anything in this world? His father died two months ago of a sudden illness, his mother is poor. The baby is a sickly child born in time of war in the middle of a harsh winter!"

"But he is a Christmas baby!" the girl said. "Surely Providence holds something special for him."

"If he lives—" the older woman observed.

The two women returned to the Newton farm. Hay stubble brittle with cold crackled under their feet. When they came through the apple orchard, they smelled smoke from the fireplace.

The farm needed repairs. Two cottages were no longer in use. Their thatched roofs leaked. The manor house had walls of gray stone with a roof of wooden shingles. Even by moonlight it showed its age.

William Ayscough, Hannah Newton's brother, had arrived from his parish in Burton Coggles. He opened the door for the two women. "Thank you for running the errand on this cold night," he said.

"The infant?" the younger woman asked anxiously.

William Ayscough's round face usually carried a calm, able expression. This morning he looked troubled. "I expect nothing will help the child now. He is in the hands of the Lord."

The two women crossed the front room. It had a low ceiling and rough stone floor. They climbed the narrow staircase to the second floor bedroom lighted by candles. Hannah Newton rested in a high, curtained bed.

Grandmother Ayscough watched over the baby. He slept in a cradle by the fire in the open hearth. She let the two women see the baby. She whispered, "He is small, and his head is much too large for his weak body."

The girl drew in her breath in wonder. "Why, he would fit in a quart jar."

The baby gave a low cry.

Hannah Newton stirred. She patted a place in the bed beside her. "Let me have the infant."

"Rest his head on a pillow," Grandmother Ayscough said as she laid the baby by his mother.

Hannah said, "Pray for my baby. He is the only son of a father who is dead. I have prayed for this child, and the Lord has granted my petition which I have made to Him."

"What will his name be?" the girl asked.

Hannah Newton said, "He will bear his father's name—Isaac Newton."

By morning neighbors gathered downstairs. James Ayscough, Hannah's other brother and the baby's uncle, read from the Bible. William Ayscough led the group in prayer. Even so, many of the neighbors thought the baby would die.

But Isaac Newton didn't die. He managed to pull through that first Christmas Day, and as the weeks passed he grew in strength.

But each day brought reports of troubles: poor crops, war, and death. Grandmother Ayscough wondered aloud, "There is blood in the wind these days. What will this child grow up to face?"

CHAPTER TWO:

"These Be Perilous Times"

Isaac grew in strength during the next two years, although he was still small for his age. The English Civil War continued to rage back and forth across the countryside, too. Royal troops under King Charles I of the Stuarts battled against men led by Oliver Cromwell and Parliament.

Woolsthorpe Manor and the Newton farm rested in the beautiful Witham River valley. But the valley could not be described as peaceful. For three years battles had rolled across Lincolnshire time and again. Because of the battles, crops were trampled down or burned. Farm animals strayed away to be taken by hungry soldiers.

Farm help could not be found. Woolsthorpe Manor fell upon difficult times. Stone walls crumbled, trees needed cutting back, and the roof leaked. Widow Newton (as the local people called her) and Grandmother Ayscough tried to keep the farm running, but two women alone could not tend the fields, and they didn't have enough money to hire farm hands.

Instead, they rented the land to nearby farmers who paid them an income of thirty pounds a year, barely enough to support the family, and not enough to halt the decline of the Manor.

"Trust God," Hannah reminded herself. "Do not worry. Pray for peace to come to this land." But she did worry about Isaac.

"He looks delicate," his grandmother said. "But he is seldom sick. Isaac Newton is a fine boy."

Hannah Newton said sadly, "But by the time he grows up there will be nothing left of Woolsthorpe Manor."

"Providence will see us through," Grandmother Ayscough said.

A few months before Isaac turned three years old a gentleman from the neighboring parish of North Witham came to call upon Widow Newton. He removed his hat and held it in his hand as if he were uneasy.

Hannah welcomed him and asked his business.

The visitor explained, "Reverend Barnabas Smith, Vicar of North Witham parish, asked me to come to you and—" The man seemed unsure of how to continue.

"Well?" Hannah urged.

The man spoke quickly. "Reverend Smith wishes to propose marriage to you."

Hannah was taken back. She grabbed the arms of the chair with both hands and leaned forward startled. "Reverend Smith must be sixty years old."

The man explained, "That is quite true. He has never thought of taking a wife before, and he has remained a bachelor. But now he is quite ready to marry. He would be well able to provide for you. He is a wealthy man." The visitor looked around the aged room with its timeworn chairs and old fixtures.

"Why does he not see me himself?" Hannah asked.

"The truth is, he is quite shy. It would be difficult for him to ask you face to face, especially if you were to be of a mind to turn him down. He has given me a day's wage to ask you in his place."

Hannah Newton's eyes grew thoughtful. "This is a most important step. You must speak with my brother James Ayscough about the matter. He will look into it for me. I will abide by his decision."

"Very well," the man said.

What would be right for Isaac? As her only child, he figured as the most important part of her plans. She read the Bible before going to sleep and prayed for God to guide her upon this important decision.

Isaac was less than three years old; even so, he could tell something important was going on about the Manor.

After a week, James Ayscough reported to his sister. James was a preacher himself, with a round face and large, easygoing eyes and a kind voice. During the week he had looked into reports about the Vicar of North Witham.

"Barnabas Smith is an honest, upright man,"

James said. "He has good reports thoughout his
parish. I believe you should consider his marriage
proposal."

Hannah thought aloud. "I want Woolsthorpe
to be restored to its rightful place as a producing
farm that would do right for Isaac. Ask Reverend
Smith to meet with us to work out a marriage con-
tract."

Barnabas Smith came to call. When his car-
riage stopped at the front of the Woolsthorpe
Manor, Hannah and James walked out and
greeted him. Isaac and Grandmother Ayscough
watched from Isaac's upstairs bedroom.

Barnabas Smith carried himself tall and upright. He had a solid face and sharp brown eyes.
He appeared to have the vigor and alertness of a
man twenty years younger.

Hannah asked, "Why do you wish me to be your
wife? We hardly know one another."

He explained, "I told friends of my desire to
marry, but I feared I would be unable to find a
good woman. The first name they mentioned was
that of Widow Newton. They told me of your
honesty and goodness."

"The same is said of you," Hannah said. "A
good man, they say, God-fearing and hard working."

Barnabas Smith's manner of speaking was formal and stiff, his speech exactly timed and measured. He looked around the farm. His lips came
together in a firm line. He disapproved of the un-
kept fields, thickly tangled hedges, and unfinished
repairs.

Woolsthorpe Manor was a tall, square building
with two floors, attic and cellar. It had lost much
of its earlier beauty. The small windows were
shuttered, the two chimneys at each end were
crumbling.

Hannah Newton followed his gaze around the farm. "It does need repairs," she agreed.

Barnabas Smith nodded. "We can work out an agreement. I will repair the manor house and add some rooms, rebuild the fences and clear the land. I will hire someone to run the farm. In addition, I will turn over a parcel of land that will bring your boy at least fifty pounds a year when he is grown."

For the first time the frown of worry lifted from Hannah's brow and she smiled at the idea of starting a new family. She had become attracted to the man before her. He had a look to his eyes, a set to his jaws, and he had clearly showed his intention of providing for her and Isaac.

Barnabas asked one thing in return. Hannah would come to North Witham to live with him, but he desired for her to leave Isaac at Woolsthorpe.

Hannah stiffened. Her face went blank with shock. "Leave Isaac behind! I wouldn't think of it."

Barnabas Smith tried to be reasonable. "My way of doing things is very strict. I am an old man and set in my ways. I am not used to strange children. It would be a strain for me, and for the boy as well, to live in a house with a stepfather."

Hannah thought about it. "Yes, Isaac has been raised by two women. As sensitive as he is, it might be difficult to accept discipline from a stepfather."

Barnabas Smith said, "If he lived here with his grandmother, you could visit him as often as you pleased. North Witham is only a mile and a half away." He smiled. "From the church tower you can see Woolsthorpe."

With a reluctant heart, Hannah agreed Barnabas might be right. Even so, she found it difficult to explain to her three-year-old child. "Some day you will understand," she whispered as she hugged him farewell.

Isaac didn't understand. He cried bitterly when she left. His sobs echoed in the big empty house. He watched at his bedroom window for her to come back. But she did not return for what seemed like a very long time to little Isaac.

But these bleak thoughts were broken by the happy sound of workmen trimming back over-grown hedges, carpenters banging on the roof, and stone masons repairing the sheep pens.

Like a flower, Woolsthorpe bloomed into new life. The musty smell was replaced by the smell of wax and furniture polish and new wood and varnish.

Grandmother Ayscough was a kindhearted woman, short and stout, with eyes that could laugh and lips that could show firm disapproval. She raised Isaac to listen to the word of God from the Bible. She taught him to give thanks for his meals and to say his prayers each night. At an early age God became important in Isaac's life.

Isaac's mother did come to see him often. A year passed, and when Isaac was four years old, his mother did not come at the expected time.

"No visit this week," Grandmother Ayscough announced.

"Why?" Isaac asked. He was helping her crush bark to make cough medicine. Isaac bit the bark. He made a face. It was sour!

"Your mother has a baby," Grandmother Ayscough explained. "A girl. Named Mary."

Even with the baby his mother had time to visit Isaac every week. At first Isaac held hurt and anger in his heart against his stepfather. He thought of terrible things which he hoped would happen to Barnabas Smith.

But all of this passed. After he began going to school, he was old enough to walk alone across the fields to his mother's home.

"Be watchful for soldiers," Grandmother Ayscough said. "Hide in the bushes if you see them coming, for these be perilous times. You won't get lost?"

"I can't get lost," Isaac said. "The steeple of the church in North Witham guides me across the fields."

Isaac enjoyed visiting with his mother and making toys for his half sister Mary and her younger brother Benjamin. He did have fun with them. He grew into a deep love for his new family.

His mother asked him about school. "How do you like it?"

Isaac shrugged. He had learned to read and write and do arithmetic problems. Otherwise, he didn't think much about school. "The other children think me peculiar because I do not speak often. I think a lot to myself."

"Do the bigger children bother you?" his mother asked.

"Not now. At first the bullies tried to make sport of me, but they gave it up when they saw they couldn't draw me into a fight."

"Good for you!" Hannah said. "What games do you play?"

Isaac admitted, "I seldom play with others. The boys are larger than I am, so I wouldn't be much fun in their games."

When the visit ended Hannah fixed his coat. She kissed him and smiled. "It is good for you to have Mary and Benjamin to love." She tucked a book under his arm. "Barnabas said for me to give this book to you."

Although books were expensive, his stepfather had one of the largest libraries around, nearly three hundred books. After this visit Isaac reminded himself to ask forgiveness in his nightly prayers for the bad things he had thought about his stepfather.

Part of the way home he heard the noise of children marching through the field and playing a wild game of soldiers. One band waved wooden swords while the other group hid behind a hedge and aimed toy muskets. They play-acted like soldiers who roamed throughout Lincolnshire looking for Royalists supporters. Only four years ago Charles I had been routed from his stronghold in Nottingham, not thirty miles away. Now the King was being held prisoner, and some said he might be beheaded.

Isaac sniffed the air. His sensitive nose told him straw was afire. He decided to investigate the smell. A few minutes later he saw the thatched roof of a barn smolder and burst into flames. Fire!

Isaac ran to the farm to help. But he pulled up short and dropped down low. Soldiers sitting on nervous horses ringed the barn. Isaac hid behind a tree to see what was up.

A farmer tried to push past the soldiers to enter

the barn. A soldier threw him back. "Your ani-mals are out. But the barn must be burned."

"Why?" the farmer asked.

"Oliver Cromwell rules England now. Those who aid the enemy must suffer."

The farmer said, "I have not aided the Royal-ists."

"A fortnight ago you allowed Royalists to hide in your barn during the day. Then at night they escaped past our patrol."

The farmer tried to explain. "They forced me—"

"Silence!" the soldier roared. His hand went to his broad sword at his side.

The flames grew hotter. Dry straw and wooden poles burned quickly. The smoke drifted to Isaac's hiding place. It burned his nose. The sting caused his eyes to water. He picked up the book and crawled back from his hiding place. He ran home to tell Grandmother Ayscough what he had seen. These were perilous times!

When Isaac arrived, Uncle James was at Wools-thorpe Manor. He directed workmen who were boarding up windows in the top floor. "The gov-ernment has passed a window tax. So we are clos-ing the top windows. It will save a few shillings a year."

Grandmother Ayscough said, "They tax the sunlight!"

Isaac could not hold back his story any longer. He told about the barn burning. "What is the war all about?" he asked.

Uncle James said, "You know about Crom-well?"

"Yes, *'Trust in God, but keep your gunpowder dry!'* " Isaac quoted the famous saying.

"That is correct. Oliver Cromwell is very strict concerning religious matters. He wears ordinary

clothes that could be the work of a country tailor.
He fines soldiers who use bad language. But there
is another side to him. Oliver Cromwell had not
even seen an army until he led his own men into
battle. He proved to be a strong general. Cromwell's men defeated the Royalists."

"But what is the fighting about?"

"Religion and government," Uncle James said.
"Whoever runs the country controls religion as
well. At first Cromwell allowed different views of
religion. Most people liked him, but today some
say he tries to force people to be good. He wants
them to believe the Bible in exactly the same way
as he does. One thing is certain, he is the most
powerful man in England."

"What will happen?" Isaac asked.

"I do not know," Uncle Ayscough said shaking
his head. "Few men who come into power can remain simple people. Never let power go to your
head, lad."

Isaac smiled at such a wild idea. Power, fame,
wealth—he hardly had to worry about that!

The off-and-on war continued. Royalists,
called Cavaliers by the local people because of
their long hair, hid in woods and marshes to make
night raids against Cromwell's men, called
Roundheads because of their short cut hair.

Long hair, short hair! It all seemed quite silly—
but frightening—to Isaac.

He attended a school in Skillington. He walked
there and back each day. When the lessons interested him, he did well. At other times he lost
himself in fancies, daydreams, and he barely
passed. Right now he looked out the window
where white thunderheads were boiling up high
in the sky.

"Attend to your work," the schoolmaster said.
He rapped the side of Isaac's desk with a cane.

Isaac wrote from the practice book:

There is no roome for me to sit.
What is hee good for?
He said nothing for feare.
I am sore afraide.

He closed the book. Children who had already finished were outside yelling to each other. Isaac gathered his books and rushed home.

"End of term!" he called to Grandmother Ayscough. "Now I will have time to hunt wild herbs for you and to draw pictures and whittle models."

Grandmother Ayscough asked, "How do you stand at school?"

"The schoolmaster said I could move up to the next form."

"In what position?" she pressed him.

"Near the bottom, I suppose. Some lessons are dull, and things that interest me are seldom taught."

"Nevertheless you will keep up your studies," Grandmother Ayscough said firmly.

"I will," Isaac agreed. "To practice writing I can copy favorite verses from the Bible—the Bible that my real father left me. For reading I have an interesting book about Daniel from stepfather Smith."

"Don't forget ciphers," Grandmother Ayscough said.

"Arithmetic? Numbers are easy because when I whittle models I figure the right size for parts."

Isaac enjoyed waking up early in the morning and walking in the woods behind the house. The gound sloped down to a small stream which ran into Witham River. It was a perfect place to walk alone and think private thoughts.

He smelled the different kinds of leaves—sweet maples, pungent elms, willows that smelled like medicine, oaks with a smell of nuts.

Wild flowers grew along the narrow, winding river. He stopped to examine a plant with tiny yellow blossoms that had a bitter smell. He crushed the leaves of another herb to release the juice: mint. His grandmother used mint leaves to make cough medicine.

He stopped to listen. Squirrels chattered in the trees. Rabbits nosed through the brush. Things moved in the grass, snakes and mice. Frogs jumped in the river when he walked nearby. In the distance a fox barked.

Thirsty? He cupped his hands to dip cool water from a bubbling spring. Everybody said the Lincolnshire springs gave the purest water in England, he thought to himself. And he agreed.

He threw out his arms in sheer joy. There was so much to see and do. "How wonderful is the world God has made!" he said aloud.

Isaac put up shelves in his room. "For my collections," he explained to Grandmother Ayscough. "I have dried flowers and shiny stones and all sorts of working models."

On the other walls he hung pictures of birds and animals that he had drawn with charcoal on brown paper. Not only did he teach himself how to draw, but he made the frames for the pictures as well.

When Uncle James saw the models his face lighted up in pleasure. He insisted that Uncle William come to see them, too. "Isaac's wooden toys of houses and carts and windmills actually move. Doors open, wheels turn, and sails spin."

Even Uncle William, calm and reserved, was impressed. As the minister for Burton Coggles parish, he was a learned man who had attended

Cambridge College.

Uncle James said, "Isaac's mind darts about like lightning flashing from a storm. His mind mops up ideas like a sponge."

Uncle William agreed. "The boy has ability. The day school has taught him as far as they can go. He must look elsewhere for a good education."

Hannah said, "Barnabas is impressed with his knowledge of Scripture. Isaac is a fine boy who is learning to let the Bible guide him. But send him to school—"

Uncle William insisted. "King's School in Grantham is the only choice."

"Seven miles!" Hannah said. "That is too far to walk."

Uncle William said, "Ralf Clark has a large home above his apothecary shop. Isaac could room with him."

Hannah sighed. She did so much want her son to make something of his life, but it hurt her for him to move farther away from her. "Very well. Next term Isaac will move to Grantham to study at King's School."

CHAPTER THREE:

King's School

Isaac rode along silently in the creaking cart, his feet on a bundle of clothes, his back resting against a crate containing his most cherished models. The cart bumped onto the cobblestone streets of Grantham.

Grantham was a small but busy town of about twelve hundred people. It had several shops, a lively market, and narrow streets rutted by the ceaseless passage of heavy farm carts bringing goods to market.

A new town, Isaac thought. A new school. A new home! How would the Clark family treat him? Would the people in the large house welcome him as a member of the family, or would they look upon him as just a boarder who brought them a little extra money each month?

Isaac said, "I've been here on market days, but I don't remember an apothecary shop."

"This is the place," Hannah said. "Mr. Clark on High Street, next door to George Inn. See the sign. The mortar and pestle show that Ralf Clark mixes medicines."

Mrs. Clark came out of the shop. Beside her stood a bright-eyed girl about the same size as Isaac but two years younger. Isaac was eleven years old, so the girl was nine.

"Catherine Storey," Hannah explained to Isaac. "She is Mrs. Clark's daughter by her first husband who died a few years ago. Catherine is the only child the Clark's have."

"Come in, Hannah," Mrs. Clark called. "Catherine, you show Isaac to his room. Gather your things and go on up."

"Will there be room for my models?" Isaac asked.

"Oh yes," the girl said. "Your room is in the attic, but there is a lot of space. Come and I will show you."

She led him to an attic bedroom that had a narrow bed, but plenty of shelves. A huge dresser with a double row of drawers and a large oak writing desk completed the simple furnishing.

The room had been recently cleaned. A candle burned on the writing table, and a checkered quilt covered the bed.

Isaac suspected the girl, so cheerful herself, had brightened the place for him. She was pretty, certainly, with sleek brown hair and brown eyes. She wore a dark blue dress with white apron, and she seemed eager for Isaac to like her.

"What beautiful toys," she said when Isaac unpacked his crate. She spun the wheel of a water mill.

"They are models, not toys," he said sternly.

"You must be very keen with tools. I have some broken toys—but I suppose they would be too difficult for you to fix."

Isaac didn't say anything.

"Would you come look? I don't have any brothers or sisters, and it is lonely to play by one-self."

Isaac couldn't resist. He unwrapped the canvas bag with his hammer and saw and other tools and went to work. Although the repairs were simple, one look in Catherine's thankful eyes when he finished made him know he had one real friend in the Clark household.

That night, after the house grew quiet, Isaac took a candle to look around the attic. In one room he found a mouse nosing around a parcel of old books. He brushed dust from the covers to read the titles. *Mathematicall Magick* by John Wilkins and *Mysteryes of Nature and Art* by John Bate. Such wonderful titles! He resolved to ask permission to read the books first thing in the morning.

Isaac awoke to the smell of breakfast. The wonderful smell of hot oats, brown sugar, and freshly baked bread drifted to his bedroom. Isaac dressed and went down.

Mrs. Clark asked, "What do you usually have for morning meal?" She wore a plain dress, simple but well cut.

Isaac said, "Hot bread and butter, and tea made of orange peels boiled in water and sweetened with sugar."

"Let me make it," Catherine said. She finished setting the table with pewter plates and a few cups of pretty china.

Ralf Clark said, "Some people say orange peels

ward off sickness during long winters."

Isaac said, "My grandmother thinks so."

Ralf Clark was a big man with a broad face and sure-looking hands. "If she is right, then I must remember to add it to my stock of remedies. High Street apothecary is the best in Lincolnshire," he said with open and honest pride.

"Will you show me around?" Isaac asked.

"Certainly," Ralf Clark agreed.

When Isaac finished breakfast, they walked along the rows of jars. Ralf Clark touched the crocks on the crowded shelves and called out the names of the contents. "White hellibore, oil of amiseeds, alum water, and purple foxglove. Each one of these is able to help improve health or cure disease."

Isaac smelled the fragrant odors of belladonna and balsam. He looked into earthenware crocks of spices and oils. He examined the vials of yellow sulphur, red cinnabar, shiny quicksilver, and rock crystals.

The chemicals fascinated Isaac. "There is so much! What are they all for? How do you know what to mix? Can I watch you work sometime?"

"Enough questions!" Ralf Clark said, although it did please him for Isaac to take an interest in the shop. "Time for school. My brother will take you to King's School."

The apothecary's brother, a physician educated at Cambridge, taught mathematics at King's School. Doctor Clark, an older man with a firm set to his jaw but an easygoing look to his eyes, gave Isaac a smile of encouragement. "A new scholar for King's School! Come along."

Isaac followed with leaden heart. School again. He would have much rather stayed behind and explored the powders, liquids, and crystals in the apothecary.

Doctor Clark said, "King's School has a good record that goes back a hundred years. Many great men have attended here. We expect our pupils to match that record."

They arrived at the building. "It looks more like a church than a school," Isaac observed.

"The playground opens onto the grounds of St. Wolfram's Church," Doctor Clark explained.

Isaac tilted back his head to look at the church steeple which soared for two hundred fifty feet in the air.

Inside, students, grouped into different forms, sat at long tables. Tutors on raised pews kept a sharp check on the activities of the students.

Doctor Clark said, "Henry Stokes is the headmaster. He is an excellent scholar and a good teacher. You will study Bible under him."

The headmaster turned out to be thin and stiff. His welcome to Isaac was formal and filled with long words. In a dry voice, a little rasping, but not unpleasant, Headmaster Stokes said, "Here is my son who is a student, too. He will set you straight about what we expect of you."

Young Stokes was a slim boy. He was thirteen years old and a head taller than Isaac. He explained the day's activity. "Important classes are in the morning: Sanderson's *Logic*, everybody studies that, followed by Latin and Scripture; then ancient history and arithmetic. At times the better students study geometry. Once or twice a week Old Barley comes in for art lessons."

Isaac nodded absent-mindedly. From his table sunlight fell against the wall. He set about trying to figure out how he could use the spot of light on the wall to measure the passage of time.

For the first few months Isaac remained a dismal student. He started at the bottom of the next to lowest form and didn't budge one place. By

day he half-heartedly studied the assigned sub-
jects, but by night he dug out the old books in the
Clark's attic and read on astronomy, botany,
chemistry, and anatomy.

However, he did do well in the Bible classes.
In a world torn apart by war and swept up in political unrest, the Bible gave Isaac the courage
and faith to look to the future.

Henry Stokes marveled at Isaac's memory. "He
can string out Bible verses from memory as if he
is reading them. Yet, his class work is extremely
poor."

"Isaac often disappears into a world of his own
making," Doctor Clark explained. "He grew up
alone on a lonely farm. That, and the fact he is
undersized has caused him to stand apart from
other students."

"Do bullies bother him much?" the headmaster
asked.

Doctor Clark said, "Normally such an undersized boy would be an attractive target for tor-
ment by other students. But his dreamy attitude
bothers them and his teachers as well. To the
other students that is a redeeming feature."

But one bully did continue to taunt Isaac. In
the past Isaac had learned how to handle rough
students. Ignore them and they would grow tired
and go away. Not this one! He enjoyed making
Isaac's life miserable. But the bully was afraid of
anybody he thought might put up a fight.

One morning the bully came toward Isaac like
a cat coming at a mouse. The loud-voiced boy
jeered Isaac. "Dumb ox!" the bully called. "Useless boy!"

He threw Isaac to the ground. The bully
kicked him in the stomach. He laughed at Isaac's
pain.

Isaac's eyes watered at the intense pain. A bit-

ter taste came to his mouth. He lay on the cold
ground and tried to get up. Throughout the day
Isaac couldn't think. His hands trembled. Never
again! Although small and timid, Isaac decided
he would fight the next time.

After school the bully again hunted out his favorite target. This time Isaac stood his ground.
He had grown up on the farm. His hands and
body could move like a whip.

"I'm going to kick you again," the bully
threatened.

"Not this time," Isaac said doggedly.

The bully looked around in surprise. Did Isaac
have help? Other students were watching, but
none of them was willing to stand up to the bully.

The fight began. Isaac put his entire mind to
the task. He stayed out of the bully's hands. Instead, Isaac rained a dozen lightning fast blows
on the bully. Isaac danced away, out of reach.

"You're not wanting to fight," the bully hedged.

Young Stokes, the schoolmaster's son, watched
the fight. If the bully talked his way out of defeat,
he would be back tomorrow taking advantage of
smaller children.

Young Stokes yelled, "He's a coward, Isaac.
Rub his nose against the wall!"

"Leave me alone," the bully panted.

Isaac grabbed his opponent by the ears and
pushed his face against the brick wall.

"You leave *me* alone!" Isaac commanded.

He released his opponent. The bully's shoulders
slumped. His whole body showed defeat. The
bully backed away and fled from his humiliation.
That was one bully who had learned his lesson!

But later Isaac felt a great deal of shame. He
had lost his temper. Isaac knew the Bible spoke
out against anger. "He that is slow to anger is
better than the mighty. . ." (Prov. 16:32). He

resolved to never again get into a fight.

He asked Catherine, "Do other students think of me as slow and stupid, like an ox?"

Catherine said, "You are often silent and dreamy."

"I think a lot to myself," Isaac explained.

Catherine teased, "That may be so. But if you are so clever, then why are you at the bottom of the next to lowest class at King's School?"

Isaac admitted, "My fancies sometimes cause me so much thought I forget my book study. But I'll beat that bully by books as well as by fist!"

Isaac had never thought about whether he had the ability to do good work. He took up the challenge. No longer would Isaac Newton be last.

He worked hard. He studied his schoolwork with a single-minded purpose and stubbornness that surprised everyone, especially his tutors at King's School. "He doesn't seem to be the same person," Headmaster Stokes said.

Each night Isaac dropped into the deep sleep of complete exhaustion. He became the master of every subject at school. He rose in class. He reached not only top in class, but top in school!

One of his favorite studies in Bible class was the book of Daniel. Isaac had learned that Daniel was a prophet. God had given Daniel the ability to understand the meaning of dreams, and he could predict future history.

"You enjoy studying the Bible," Catherine said.

Isaac said, "Yes. In a time with war the Bible is a comfort. Like arithmetic, it gives answers that are either yes or no, right or wrong. There is no middle ground. Have you read the poem I wrote?"

He took out a piece of paper, unfolded it, and handed it to her.

"I cannot read very well," Catherine said.

"You read it to me."

"Oh," Isaac said. Everything she knew had been taught to her at home. "I will read it. Maybe you can give it a title:

A secret art my soul requires to try,
If prayers can give me, what the wars deny.
Three crowns distinguish'd here in order do
Present their objects to my knowing view.
Earth's crown, thus at my feet, I can disdain,
Which heavy is, and, at the best, but vain.
But now a crown of thorns I gladly greet,
Sharp is this crown, but not so sharp as sweet.
A crown of glory that I yonder see
Is full of bliss and of eternity."

Catherine said, "It's beautiful. Will you make me a copy?"

"Yes," Isaac said. "You are my very best friend. I'm lucky to board with your family. Your mother cooks food especially for me and treats me like her very own son. Your father teaches me about medicine and chemistry."

Isaac had begun to keep a notebook to record his wide–ranging interests. *Isaac Newton owns this book*, he wrote inside his first notebook. "There is so much to learn," he said to Ralf Clark. "From now on I intend to copy down everything I find interesting."

He read to Catherine from his notebooks, "Here is how to make a paint that gives the color of the sea: Take privet berries and dry them in the sun. Then crush them and steep them in alum water and strain them in an earthen porringer that is glazed."

"You have notes about everything," Catherine said. "How do you manage to stay first in the class?"

"Sometimes I forget to work enough with my books, and a student overtakes me," Isaac admitted. "Then I put aside my contraptions and outstrip my rival."

Ralf Clark said, "Henry Stokes looks upon you with the pride of a father. You're his favorite pupil."

Isaac smiled. His school work had not dimmed his interest in models. "Right now I am making a model of the Gunnerby Road windmill," he said.

Isaac enjoyed watching the millwrights at their work. They were putting up a new windmill on the road between Gunnerby and Grantham. "Here are my drawings of it," Isaac said. "My model will be exactly like it except in size."

"Will it work?" Catherine asked.

He looked at her with calm assurance. "Everything I make works."

By now Isaac had changed his attic room into a workshop, filled with saws and hammers and all kinds of gadgets.

Catherine came to watch as he put finishing
touches on the windmill. Isaac leaned far out
the attic window to attach the windmill to the
roof of the house. Then he and Catherine ran
downstairs and out into the street.

"Look!" Catherine yelled with glee. "The wind
is turning the sails. It works!"

Later, Isaac brought the windmill back inside.
He hooked up a mouse to turn it, and put grains
of wheat under the miniature grinding stones.
The mouse ground the wheat into flour.

"But your miller eats up all the profits!"
Catherine laughed.

Another of Isaac's inventions was more practical. He made tiny lanterns of crinkled paper
with candles inside. He used them to light his
way to school during the dark mornings during
winter.

The paper lanterns gave him an idea. "I've
always wanted to see a comet," Isaac said to
Catherine, "like the one your father told me
about. But so far I've been unlucky."

A bright comet is one of the most frightful of
all celestial objects. A comet looks like a giant
star, but as it sweeps into view, a long tail glows
with a strange silver light. Many people feared
the sight of a new comet. It looked too much like
a silver sword about to strike the earth.

Isaac said, "Unlike the planets, no one can predict when a comet will flash into view."

"What can you do about it?" Catherine asked.

Isaac pointed to an extra large kite in the corner. "Tonight I'll make a comet. I'll use this
kite to fly a lantern in the night sky. It will be
a spectacular sight!"

"Oh, let me go with you," Catherine said.

"Good," Isaac agreed. "You can help me

launch the kite."

The night was beautiful and crisp, with a crescent moon glowing over the sleeping landscape with a soft yellow light. Isaac waited until the moon set and the night turned completely black.

He fixed up the kite with its paper lantern and sent the kite soaring into the night sky. The kite disappeared into the darkness. Under it an eerie light floated in the sky, darting and dancing around.

Isaac and Catherine heard the startled cry of townspeople. "A comet!" one man cried. "Danger is upon us!"

"The people are afraid," Catherine said. "They think this is a real comet. Comets are supposed to tell of the coming of terrible events."

"But that's a silly superstition," Isaac said. "God uses simple rules to run His kingdom."

But the strange light in the night sky had alarmed the townspeople and almost caused a panic. "I can't understand why it would frighten people," Isaac said.

Ralf Clark explained, "When people do not understand something, they are afraid of it."

When Isaac was thirteen and into his second year at King's School, he learned that his step-father Barnabas Smith had died.

Ralf Clark said, "He must have thought a great deal of you because he left his entire library of three hundred books to you."

"Mother?" Isaac wondered. "What will she do?"

"Move back to the farm at Woolsthorpe, I would think," Ralf Clark said. "When you are older, she will need your help to run the farm."

"No more school?" Isaac asked. His earlier dislike of school had changed. Now he wanted to stay in Grantham and go to King's School.

"Oh, it will be a year or so before your mother gets settled in and will need your help. Make that time count."

Isaac filled the time left to him with reading, making models, mixing chemicals for the apothecary and studying the Bible. There never seemed to be enough time to do the things that he wanted to do.

Soon after he turned fifteen he returned to the Clark family after a weekend visit to Woolsthorpe.

"It's all over," Isaac said sadly. "Mother wants me to carry on the business of the farm."

"Your mother needs the help of her eldest son," Ralf Clark explained, but he saw the sadness in Isaac's eyes. "But you will always be welcome here. Visit me whenever you are in Grantham. Borrow any of my books that interest you."

Isaac found it difficult to say good-bye to Catherine. "There is still so much I want to do: books to read, models to make, investigations into medicine and chemistry to carry out. However, Mother has waited as long as she can. I must go."

"Good-bye," Catherine said. Tears were in her eyes, too.

CHAPTER FOUR:

Hawk Among the Sparrows

With Hannah Smith at Woolsthorpe were her three children from her marriage to Barnabas Smith: Mary, age eleven; Benjamin, age eight; Hannah, six years old.

"How is it to be home?" his mother asked.

"It's a livelier place," Isaac observed. "And noisier." The children seemed to dash all over the place, and he feared his models would soon be broken like common toys.

His mother said, "We have enough money to live in comfort, but I need your help with the chores. Those quiet years as a Pastor's wife in North Witham have made it difficult to settle back into running Woolsthorpe as I did when you were a baby."

"I will do the best I can," Isaac said. He meant exactly what he said.

Hannah nodded. "You are sixteen years old now, and it is time for you to begin to take on the duties as head of the household. Soon you will be master of the Manor."

Isaac's head reeled at such a thought. As head of the Manor he would sit as judge over disputes between farmers in the area. He would run the entire Woolsthorpe estate.

Times continued to be difficult. Two Civil Wars had brought disaster to the Lincolnshire countryside. Oliver Cromwell became the Lord Protector, the most powerful man in England. He soon became impatient with people who refused to do his bidding. He ruled with the iron hand of a dictator.

"Cromwell's troops are everywhere," Uncle James reported. "They control worship in the church buildings; they decide what should be taught in the schools, and they enforced their brand of justice in the courts."

In his own mind Isaac had formed his own ideas about freedom of religion. It seemed to him that no outside source should force people to believe in a special way. The Bible, as the Word of God, told the truth; yet, every person would have to read and study the Bible for himself. The Bible showed what God wanted His people to do.

Right now, however, his thoughts returned to the problem of learning how to run Woolsthorpe Manor. Although he wanted to be a successful farmer, his mind wandered. The chores were so simple. It took no mental ability to watch sheep or walk behind the ox plowing the field. Neither did pitching hay, threshing grain or salting meat.

Time and again his mind wandered. Isaac never intentionally left undone his farm duties. Instead, more exciting matters captured his attention. Farming suffered.

Some chores he did enjoy, such as repairing

carts and checking animals for disease. His favorite task came on Wednesday when he left the farm to go into Grantham on business.

For two hundred years farmers had set aside Wednesday to come to Grantham to sell their produce or trade for the products they needed.

Hannah Smith sent an old and trusted servant with Isaac. She explained to the servant: "Instruct Isaac in the business of buying and selling. He must develop skill in talking down the prices and interesting buyers in our goods. You are the man to show him how."

Each Wednesday the two would ride into town and put up their horses at Saracen's Head Inn near Westgate, then go to the noisy market.

Farmers led sleepy-eyed oxen. Young boys rode well-groomed horses that pranced about. Milkmaids stood watch over pens of chickens and ducks. Tanners sold leather goods. Craftsmen displayed expensive iron tools.

Isaac liked market day because it gave him a chance to visit the Clarks. As quickly as possible he finished the farm business. Then he slipped away to visit the apothecary shop.

After a few months, the hired servant reported sadly to Mrs. Smith. "May I beg your pardon, ma'am," he said. "But young Isaac is not meant to be a farmer."

She was taken back. "And why would that be?" Hannah asked. "Isaac has a sharp mind."

The servant explained, "But he doesn't have the kind of mind farming takes. Isaac is too straightforward. Trading must be done in a roundabout way. Isaac looses interest too quickly."

"What do you suggest?" Hannah Smith asked.

The servant said, "I will carry on the farm business when we go to Grantham. Young Isaac can go to the apothecary shop. That is the way it should be. He will learn more there than at the market."

"But he will not learn how to buy sheep or sell barley," Hannah said. Reluctantly she agreed to the servant's plan.

From then on, as soon as Isaac and the hired servant reached the market, Isaac hurried over to High Street to the apothecary. He climbed to the attic. He pulled out old books and sat by the window reading them. Once again he delighted in the wonderful diagrams in *The Mysteries of Art and Nature* by John Bate.

Isaac purchased a notebook small enough to carry with him. He copied from the books. He jotted down descriptions of birds and minerals. He learned about chemistry and art.

Isaac painted a picture for Catherine using paints he mixed himself.

"The gold color is so beautiful," Catherine said. "How do you make it?"

Isaac read from his notebook. "This requires a freshly laid egg with a small hole in one end. After shaking out the white, but being careful to leave the yolk, one must pour mercury into the shell."

Catherine interrupted. "Mercury is one of the chemicals in our shop."

Isaac nodded. "The hole is then sealed with wax and the egg is placed under a setting hen. Several weeks later, the egg is opened and the contents mixed well. Gold ink! I have the egg with me." He dipped a quill in it for her to mark with.

"It writes beautifully," she agreed.

"Watch," he said. He took the egg and covered it with a handkerchief. When he tossed the handkerchief into the air, the egg had vanished.

"Oh!" Catherine squealed. "How did you do that!"

"No great mystery," Isaac said. "It is a slight of hand trick. See! The egg is in my other hand. Whenever I learn a new trick, I write it in my notebook."

"Your notebook must contain something about everything," Catherine said.

"Almost," Isaac agreed. "Here are problems in trigonometry and navigation, ideas about short-hand and spelling, and how to make a sundial and water clock."

Catherine marveled. "How do you pack so much into such a small book?"

"I've developed a system of shorthand that lets me write two hundred words on a single page," he explained.

"Have you written another poem?" she asked.

"Yes," Isaac said. "Here is one with the title 'When Jesus Saw the Cross.'"

Isaac enjoyed being with Catherine. When he came to visit her, he brought special treats: cherry tarts and custards.

Mrs. Clark spoke to her husband one day after Isaac left. "I expect Isaac and Catherine intend to marry."

Ralf Clark said, "Isaac is too steady a lad to think about that until he has a dependable income. He knows he will never be a successful farmer. I expect he will become a minister."

Mrs. Clark said, "Catherine must begin to save for her dowry. A young lady is expected to have enough to set a table and furnish the house when she marries."

Ralf Clark laughed, "Headmaster Stokes is working to make Isaac a scholar; his mother is training him as a farmer, and you are planning upon getting him married!"

Back at Woolsthorpe Manor, Isaac turned his room into a workshop like the one in the attic of the Clark home. But now he tried to make more practical contraptions such as tools and time-keepers.

He drove wooden pegs into the outside wall of the house. His sister Mary asked about the pegs in the wall.

"A sundial," he explained.

"What will you do on cloudy days?" Mary asked. "How will you tell time then?"

Isaac thought a moment. "A water clock is the answer," he decided.

"Do you know how to make one?" Mary asked. "Clocks are rare and very expensive."

Isaac explained, "John Bate's book tells how to make a water clock that keeps accurate time."

The clock worked because water dripped through a small hole in a bowl at the top of the clock into a second bowl at the bottom. As the level of the water raised in the bottom bowl a board floated higher. The floating board pushed up a stick which turned a gear and moved the hand around the clock face. At that time clocks only had one hand, the hour hand. Minute hands were not used.

Isaac finished the four-foot high water clock and outfitted it in a handsome case. Instead of winding the clock each morning, he emptied the bottom bowl and refilled the top bowl with water. The clock worked!

During this time instruments such as clocks, compasses, thermometers, and telescopes were taking the guesswork out of scientific investigations.

Torricelli, an Italian student of Galileo, invented a barometer which used a glass tube filled with mercury to measure air pressure. Torricelli believed the height of mercury in the tube indicated the type of weather to expect.

During the early part of 1658 his barometer showed a sudden drop in air pressure, far greater than he had ever seen before. Torricelli predicted a storm was at hand. His forecast came true. A terrible storm swept throughout England and Europe.

Isaac Newton, on the farm when the storm struck, rushed out to check the animals in the barn and to bolt the door and lock the shutters.

On the way to the barn he became fascinated by the force of the wind. Trees broke and limbs flew through the air. Lightning flashed. Thunder rumbled. The wind roared.

Everyone was terrified, except Isaac. The storm interested him too much for him to be afraid.

Hannah grew worried. The ten-minute chore had turned into an hour's absence. She went into the fierce storm to look for her son. The heavy barn door blew back and forth. The wind twisted it from its hinges.

Where was Isaac? There, she saw him jumping into the air. "Whatever are you doing at a time like this?" She yelled to be heard above the howling wind.

"Ah," Isaac said, his mind working, "A book I read said wind has a force to it, and the book is right. I can measure the force by jumping into it. Watch!"

He jumped into the storm against the wind. He marked his landing place with a stone and then turned to jump with the wind. "After this I can see how far the wind blows me to judge the strength of a storm."

"Come in," Hannah said, "before the storm blows you away altogether."

When the storm passed, it had taken away

many old landmarks around the country: ancient trees were uprooted, chimneys were toppled, and buildings were torn apart.

Later, Hannah told friends how she found her son happily experimenting in the middle of one of the most frightening storms in memory.

She said, "He has a head for figures and a hand for making repairs . . . but he has too many fancies to occupy his mind. . . ."

"He daydreams!" Mary said. "Yesterday he came in with a faraway look in his eyes and a bridle dragging along behind him. He had been walking the horse and it slipped the bridle. He walked in with the bridle—and never noticed that the horse was missing!"

"He is what God has made him," Uncle James observed. "He'll be just that regardless of whether he tries to be a farmer or a sailor or tradesman. His tutors at King's School spent four years training him to read and think and learn. You can't expect him to put that aside in a few months."

"But it has been two years!" Hannah cried.

"And he may need another two years, or even more."

"No," Hannah said. "He comes from a long line of farmers. What else can he do?"

Uncle James said, "When you try to train a hawk to fly with the sparrows, don't expect an easy time."

Actually, Isaac's interest in nature was directly related to his interest in the Bible. He believed the order in the universe had been put there by God. Isaac firmly believed that in studying the laws of nature he was learning more about God.

Scientific investigation uncovered the wonderful design put in the universe by the Creator's hand. Later, when Isaac learned that some men

faked experiments he looked upon it as a terrible
sin. Faked experiments lied about God's creation.

The Bible was Newton's favorite book. By this
time many people realized that Isaac was an ex-
ceptional student of the Bible. He knew it as
well as most preachers.

Isaac believed the Bible was meant to be read.
Throughout the years he grew in his conviction
that every person should read the Bible and from
it learn about God's plan.

Oliver Cromwell, who had made religious freedom difficult, suddenly became ill. Some said
the storm, like a comet, foretold the coming of a
terrible event. Some of the superstitious supporters of Cromwell believed the storm warned of
the death of their ruler.

In fact, the ailing Cromwell did grow weaker.
He died a few days after the storm. His son took
over, but the people were tired of the troubles
and trials of the Civil War period. In 1660, they
welcomed King Charles II back from exile in
Europe to sit upon the throne of England.

The tall, handsome King promised religious
toleration and a general pardon to the followers
of Cromwell. Enthusiastic crowds were on hand
at Dover to greet the monarch. A general feeling
of good will spread throughout the land.

Uncle William Ayscough, the minister at Burton Coggles, believed the time had come for Hannah to send Isaac back to school. Even the stern,
white-headed Uncle William saw Isaac was
wasted on the farm.

He explained to Hannah, "Today, on my journey here, I noticed the sheep straying from the
field. Upon looking closer I found Isaac curled
up under the hedge. He was busy with a problem from a book on mathematics. While he figured the size of the field, sheep strayed from the

meadow."

Hannah sighed and shook her head sadly. "It hasn't turned out the way I had hoped. Each day he wakes up with determination to be a model farmer. But it doesn't last."

Uncle William said, "It appears Providence has made Isaac to be a scholar, perhaps even a minister. He is capable of going to Cambridge. His mind is sharper than a two–edged sword."

Hannah said, "You certainly see more in him than most people do. Still, it is a pleasant idea that Isaac might amount to something greater than this farm has to offer."

She smiled, "I have grown weary of trying to make my hawk fly with the sparrows."

Uncle William said, "Headmaster Stokes strongly recommends that Isaac return to finish at King's School. He says it would be a great loss to the world to bury so promising a genius in country employment. And such an attempt would be vain anyway because it is clear that farming opposes Isaac's natural temperament."

Hannah sighed, "I haven't the money."

"Providence will provide," Uncle William said. "Henry Stokes is so anxious for Isaac to finish King's School he will set aside the tuition of forty shillings per term."

"What then?" Hannah asked. "Isaac would not have the money to enter Cambridge."

Uncle William, who had attended Cambridge himself to prepare for the ministry, said, "Provided Isaac is a good scholar he will not be turned away."

Once again Hannah found herself agreeing to send Isaac off to King's School. This time she knew he would not return to the farm. Within a year he graduated at the top of the school. Then, on to Cambridge!

CHAPTER FIVE:

Scholars and Scoundrels

During a warm, sunny day on June 5, 1661, Isaac climbed aboard the stage coach which would take him the fifty-five miles to Cambridge University where he would enroll at Trinity College. The trip across extremely bad roads would not be a simple outing. They had to watch for the ever-present danger of highway robbers.

Of course, highwaymen would have poor pickings if they robbed Isaac. He had with him only a bundle of clothing and the old Bible his father had left him.

Two days later the coachman pulled up the horses in front of the White Lion Tavern. Isaac dismounted and walked along the narrow streets of the bustling town to the River Cam. There he turned down Cambridge Street and strolled along until he came to the Great Gate of the University.

All along the way Isaac spotted students. It

was easy to recognize students. They wore long gowns and flat, mortarboard hats. They laughed and talked as they weaved in and out of shops and taverns.

A student who had been drinking too much bumped into Isaac. Isaac, shocked, stepped aside. Each of the fifteen or so colleges that made up Cambridge University had gowns with their own distinctive colors. This scholar bore the colors of Trinity College. He was supposed to be in training as a clergyman. Isaac shook his head sadly.

Uncle William had pulled Isaac aside the day he finished at King's School. "Congratulations upon graduation at the head of your class," Uncle William had said. "You have been accepted at Cambridge as a Sizar. Socially, it is the lowest standing. You will pay for your room and board by doing chores for your tutor and serving the professors their meals."

"I understand," Isaac said.

Uncle William said, "Maybe you do. However, let me warn you about students who will look down their noses at a lowly farm boy. You haven't well-known relatives or rich friends to ease you along the way."

"I will make it," Isaac resolved.

"Very well," Uncle William had said. "Here is a letter of introduction. Present it to Dr. Ferne as soon as you arrive. He is the Master of Trinity. He will explain your duties as Sizar and assign you a room."

Dr. Ferne turned out to be an harassed man who rushed through the interview with Isaac. "You are only one of forty-five new students coming to Trinity this session," Dr. Ferne explained. "Your tutor is Senior Fellow Benjamin Pulleyn. He will explain your duties as Sizar. My clerk will show you to your quarters."

Dr. Ferne waved a hand of dismissal. This certainly could not be described as a warm welcome!

Three of the new students were Sizars. Very soon Isaac learned that a Sizar's day began with the first light of dawn. He arose while his roommate slept and rushed to the dining hall to prepare breakfast for the professors.

He hastily ate breakfast in the kitchen while he filled a tray with food for Benjamin Pulleyn. When the professor finished eating, Isaac cleared the table. With one ear he listened for the bell calling him to the first lecture.

At noon Isaac raced back to the dining hall, his long gown flapping as he sprinted across campus. He arrived in time to serve the noon meal. He served lunch and grabbed a bite for himself while he cleared the table.

When the afternoon classes ended, Isaac made himself ready to do chores for Professor Pulleyn. He polished shoes, delivered messages, and ran errands into town. Isaac had to be careful to be back to the kitchen in time to serve supper.

When the professors left the dining hall, Isaac made a meal from the food remaining on the table. His food came from the servings left uneaten on the table.

Now, with it growing dark outside, Isaac had time to spend a few minutes at the library. With such an exacting schedule, it is little wonder that there was nothing outstanding about Isaac's college work during his first years at Trinity. To his instructors he was only another face in the lecture hall.

At the end of the day Isaac lighted a candle and settled down to study. Unfortunately, Trinity was overcrowded. Isaac shared a room with another student who was fond of giving wild parties. The parties lasted until morning hours.

Isaac found it impossible to study. He felt ill at ease in the same room with the richly dressed young man and his witty and fashionable friends. In turn, they were uneasy to be around a boy more interested in book learning than in fun and games.

Isaac wrote a letter home to Uncle William: *Loving Uncle*:

It is commonly reported about how things have changed at Trinity since you were a student here. I am sorry to report it is true. Like the rest of the country, Cambridge has fallen into hard times.

The best teachers escaped to Europe to avoid the unrest during the Civil Wars, and the Uni-

versity is badly disorganized. Discipline is relaxed. Although the University is supposed to train clergymen, sports and social life seem to have become more important than studies.

The strict religious training that Cromwell began fell apart when Charles II gained the throne. The notorious looseness of morals in his court has spread to London and from there to Cambridge.

If it please God, this pitiful time will pass and the University will get back to the business of training students in the study of Scripture—which is man's proper study.

Your very loving nephew
I. N.

One night Isaac's roommate returned to their chambers after the taverns had closed. The roommate set up a table for a night of gambling at cards and hard drinking.

The room filled with the haze of tobacco smoke and the smell of ale. Isaac gave up the struggle to study. He shook his head. Why do they waste their time? He left the room in favor of a walk out in the cool night air. He strolled to the fountian in the Great Court of the College.

Isaac heard footsteps behind him. He turned to see another student walking across the Great Court toward him. The other student seemed dejected. Isaac became curious.

"Why do you walk about at this late hour?" Isaac asked.

The other student sighed. "A wild roommate is making my life miserable. I am unable to sleep, and just as unable to study. My roommate studies in jest and plays in earnest."

Isaac smiled grimly at the old joke. "I know

what you mean. My name is Isaac Newton and I'm a Sizar."

The other boy said, "John Wickins is my name. I'm studying for the ministry—at least I'm trying to study."

Isaac knew what he meant. "Too many friends, too much money. That is the problem with my roommate."

"You are describing the student I lodge with!" John Wickins cried. "Wait! If they are so alike, then maybe one would agree to switch rooms. We would be left sharing a room together well away from the noise. Are you agreeable?"

Isaac jumped up in excitement. "What a wonderful idea. I have been praying for an answer to this problem."

"You talk with your roommate, and I'll speak to mine," John Wickins said as they shook hands.

John Wickins's fast-living roommate was happy to make the change. Isaac moved his belongings up the narrow stairs to John Wickins's second-floor room.

As the months passed the Bible-loving John Wickins became Isaac's best friend at Trinity. Before this Isaac had been terribly homesick. Now the trips home to the warm, family atmosphere of Woolsthorpe were not as often as before.

Whenever Isaac visited home he never failed to ride into Grantham to talk with bright-eyed Catherine. She always succeeded in raising his spirits.

"What are you studying now?" she asked when he came calling during the spring break of 1662.

"My days are much the same. Beside my duties as Sizar, I study Latin, Greek, the Bible, arithmetic, and logic. The first session did not carry any science classes. Now, however, I have lectures in astronomy and mathematics, such as they are."

"You appear disappointed," Catherine observed.

Isaac explained. "The professors stand before the class and read from books written by ancient Greek writers who lived two thousand years ago. The discoveries of modern scientists such as Copernicus and Galileo are ignored."

Catherine said, "It must be very trying to sit and listen while someone reads from a book."

Isaac agreed. "Although Professor Pulleyn says all examples of wisdom and human folly have been perfectly illustrated by classic writers, I believe learning should be something more than saying, 'Ptolemy said this,' or 'Aristotle said that.'"

"We students must not only read the approved books, but we must memorize the answers from them as well." This bothered Isaac. The Bible and it alone was the basic source of Christian conduct. The classics were required reading, yet they were written by pagans who had not known of the Holy Scriptures.

"The college library is pitifully small, and all it contains are old books. When a person wants an answer to a question, he doesn't solve it by experiments. No! He looks it up in Aristotle.

"Why, Aristotle lived three hundred years before Christ was born, yet nobody thinks of questioning his books or putting his statements to the test. If Aristotle says it is true, then the matter is settled.

"Even when a professor does set up a demonstration, it is performed by assistants. The teacher looks on from a high desk and directs the assistants by reading from the books of the ancients."

Isaac tried to hide his displeasure; these careless, half-hearted demonstrations proved nothing. If the facts and the book didn't agree, the professors said it was the facts that were in error!

CHAPTER SIX

Science in Newton's Time

Isaac had grown up making models and building instruments such as clocks and sundials. He knew there was much to be discovered through practical experiments. But the teachers of his time thought it beneath their dignity to work with their hands like common laborers.

Isaac Newton reflected, "Galileo died the same year I was born. Trinity needs a teacher with Galileo's skill, someone who teaches an up-to-date science."

Newton knew the proper study of nature would be difficult. Too many old-fashioned scientists objected to new ways. Galileo, for example, fought all of his life to have the errors removed from the books of Aristotle.

Aristotle had written, "An iron ball that weighs one hundred pounds that falls from a height of one hundred cubits reaches the ground before a one-pound ball has fallen a single cubit."

In other words, a ball one hundred times as

heavy falls one hundred times as fast.

By Galileo's time, some scientists figured this idea might be false; however, no one dared to question Aristotle's books aloud—until Galileo came along.

A rumor sprang up that Galileo embarrassed the entire Pisa Faculty by dropping different size iron balls from the tower of Pisa. Both the heavy and the light iron balls struck the ground at the same time. Aristotle was wrong!

Galileo showed how foolish the professors were to blindly accept the writings of the ancients.

"Who can assure us that everything that can be known in the world is known already?" Galileo asked. "Who can set bounds to man's understanding?"

The professors were furious that a mere eighteen-year-old had shown how utterly wrong they were. They made his life so miserable he left the university in 1585. He moved to the University of Padua—where he fared even worse!

Astronomy was one of Isaac's favorite studies, so he read with interest the discoveries Galileo made at Padua. While there Galileo learned of a "magnifying tube," or telescope, which had the power to make distant things appear near at hand.

Galileo instantly saw that the telescope could be used to study the heavens.

According to Aristotle, the heavens were perfect, without blemish. The earth alone was irregular and disorderly. Aristotle taught that the moon was a perfect ball and the sun smooth and polished.

Galileo made a telescope and turned it to the moon. He discovered mountains, craters, plains, and deep valleys. The moon was as rugged and uneven as the earth itself. The ancient writers were proven wrong again!

Jealous professors charged Galileo with all sorts
of crimes. They even said he spoke against the
Bible.

The charge was a lie. Galileo had studied both
the Bible and the heavens, and he had become
even more convinced that only a Creator could
have set the solar system in motion.

Galileo said, "The Holy Scriptures are intended
to teach men how to go to heaven, not how the
heavens go. Look through my telescope."

Isaac could hardly believe it, but some professors refused to look through Galileo's telescope!
They were afraid he might prove them wrong.

In his lectures, Galileo explained his own discoveries and described how Johannes Kepler had
worked out three simple laws that summarized
the complex motions of the planets.

Galileo said, "It is possible that all motions,
both on earth and in the heavens, can be predicted by the use of simple laws which have not
yet been brought to light."

Galileo failed to find the universal law of motion.

When Isaac Newton returned to Trinity to begin the fall session of 1662, no one seemed to be
any nearer to a solution. But during his vacation
Isaac had read and mastered Johannes Kepler's
book.

John Wickins greeted Isaac to their chambers.
His eyes were all alight with barely concealed
pleasure.

"A surprise," Isaac guessed.

"Right," John Wickins said. "Guess who is coming to Trinity to teach. Doctor Isaac Barrow!"

Isaac Newton knew the name. "Doctor Isaac
Barrow of Gresham College in London."

"That is correct. He is outstanding in many
ways." John Wickins said. "Ten years ago Doctor

Barrow graduated from Trinity. The political trouble was at its highest, so Doctor Barrow decided to take a long trip through Europe and to the Holy Land.

"On the way to Symrna, Algerian pirates attacked the ship. Doctor Barrow manned a gun and helped drive away the pirates. He is a very remarkable man."

Isaac said, "You're always talking about what a great preacher he is."

John Wickins said, "King Charles calls him the finest preacher in England. When he finishes a sermon there is nothing else to add about the subject. I have several books of his sermons. Oh! If only I could preach as he does!"

"Now you will be able to attend his lectures," Isaac said.

"No, I am sorry to say. But my loss is your gain."

"How do you mean?" Isaac asked.

"Doctor Barrow will teach mathematics and natural science."

Isaac remembered now. Doctor Barrow was considered an exceptionally brilliant mathematician. "I must become one of his students," Isaac resolved.

Soon after the Easter term opened, Isaac began meeting classes with Doctor Barrow. It was a great honor to be accepted as a student of the great Doctor Barrow.

Physically, Doctor Barrow was very strong, with the courage to match, although he was rather small in size. He had a lean figure, calm manner, and clear, gray eyes.

Once, while leaving a friend's house a fierce mastiff dog, one of the most dangerous animals known, broke his chain and charged at Doctor Barrow.

Doctor Barrow had the courage to take the dog by the throat. With a mighty struggle he forced the dog to the ground. He held it there until help arrived.

The students at Trinity told a story about Isaac Barrow when he was a child. He had been restless and hard to control. He was a problem child. His father once said that if it pleased God to take any of his children to heaven, his son Isaac could best be spared.

Although a great scientist and forceful teacher, Doctor Barrow's main interest centered upon the study of the Bible and bringing its message to the people.

"What is the purpose of life?" Doctor Barrow asked. "It is to learn God through His works. The greatest error a natural philosopher makes is to think his success is due to his own ability. God is the creator of all things, even success."

Isaac listened spellbound as Doctor Barrow described his adventures in the Holy Land. They spent interesting hours after class talking about many things.

Ralf Clark had been like a father to Isaac. Now Doctor Barrow became a brother to Isaac.

"A scholar must have a balanced education," Doctor Barrow said. "Otherwise he will have a poor base upon which to study."

Isaac kept silent. He often let some of his studies lapse in order to study what interested him the most.

Doctor Barrow asked, "Why have you not studied Euclid's *Geometry?*"

Newton turned down his hand. "Euclid's *Geometry* is too easy. There is no reason to study it."

"You will see otherwise some day," Doctor Barrow warned.

In 1664, three years after he entered Trinity, Newton applied for a scholarship. If he passed the test, he could drop his job as Sizar and spend more of his time in study.

Three teachers interviewed him. One was Doctor Barrow. When his time came to ask questions, he pounced upon Isaac's lack of study in Euclid.

Isaac, so sure of himself, his head in the air, suddenly found himself stumbling through the questions. He grew red with embarrassment.

Newton received the scholarship, but he had learned his lesson. Soon Doctor Barrow could point to Isaac as one of Trinity's finest students of geometry.

One day John Wickins unexpectedly plucked a hair from Isaac's head. "You spend too much time studying," he said playfully. "See, your hair is turning white."

Isaac inspected the hair. He joked, "It is not due to my studies at all, but my experiments with quicksilver."

Whatever the cause, his hair began to change, and while still a young man Isaac Newton sported a full head of hair, completely white.

Doctor Barrow lectured upon experiments with light and telescopes. Newton was keenly interested in astronomy, and he desired to have a telescope of his own, but he could not afford one.

Doctor Barrow encouraged him. "You can make a telescope. I will instruct you in the way to grind lenses."

Isaac had always been fascinated by ingenious scientific apparatus. He set to work with a will. "It feels good to again be using my hands."

He enjoyed the gritty sound of glass grinding, the red optical rouge, the satin feel of glass polished to a smooth finish.

Isaac mounted the lenses in a long paper tube. John Wickins examined it as Isaac braced it against the window frame of their room.

Isaac said, "It is like the one Galileo made except for the eyepiece which is modeled after Kepler's design."

Although his roommate seemed quite impressed, Isaac wasn't satisfied with the telescope's performance. True, it showed the mountains and craters of the moon, the phases of Venus, and the moons of Jupiter. But a band of colors, like a rainbow, circled each bright object.

"What is the matter," Isaac asked Doctor Barrow. "The image of bright objects is circled by a bothersome ring of colors."

"Very observant of you," Doctor Barrow said. "No one knows the exact reason for the rainbow."

"Can't anything be done?" Isaac asked.

"Christian Huygens in Holland is the most skilled telescope maker in the world. Even he is unable to remove the unwanted color."

During the winter of 1664 a great comet came into view. Isaac threw a cloak over his shoulders and set out to a hilltop to watch it. The comet traveled a lonely path through the heavens. He watched the flickering light as it swam through the cold, dark sky.

A bright comet! He still remembered his kite-made comet. Now he became a careful observer of this real-life comet. He spent hours on the hilltop near the college. Night after night Isaac recorded the comet's position. The comet seemed to waver, like a frosty wind, a ghostly shadow flickering through the stars.

"I plotted its orbit," he explained to Doctor Barrow. "But it seems to have a mind of its own."

Doctor Barrow said, "Predicting the exact path of a comet is a very difficult scientific problem. Comets do not seem to follow the rules of most heavenly bodies."

On December 4, the comet made its closest approach to the sun. Newton tried time and again to predict its exact path. But the comet refused to follow the path Isaac had calculated.

"Don't charge the failure to your calculations," Doctor Barrow said. "No one has been able to calculate its orbit. We need a new sort of mathematics."

The great mathematicians, Copernicus, Kepler, Galileo, and Descartes, had worked upon developing a better form of mathematics. Isaac read their books again.

Late one night he announced to his roommate,

"The best hope seems to be Rene Descartes. He invented a new type of geometry in which equations and number sentences replaced lines and figures. With it, geometry problems can be solved by using arithmetic instead of drawing figures on paper."

John Wickins said, "Descartes? He's the Frenchman who spoke against Aristotle's iron-clad hold on logic. But his ideas are not in favor very well here at Trinity."

Isaac agreed. "I found quite a stir against him in my logic class. The professor told us not to read his books. The professor railed against Descartes and talked as if he speaks against the very Gospel."

"Well, you have struggled with the comet problem enough for one night," John Wickins suggested.

"No," Isaac said. "No sleep tonight. I am going out to plot the comet's position more accurately."

John Wickins awoke to find the other bed had not been slept in. The door opened and Isaac stumbled into the room. He appeared weak. His eyes had a faraway look in them. His clothes were ill-kept, his face gray.

"You're ill," John Wickins cried out in alarm.

Isaac fumbled around for his books. "I must be going to lectures," he whispered.

"No," John Wickins said. "Lie down." He helped Isaac to the bed.

"I can't sleep," Isaac protested. "I haven't slept in five days."

"Then rest!" John said sternly. "You have over-worked yourself."

For days Isaac laid in the bed, his face to the wall, his mind blank.

John carried broth to the room and fed him. Slowly, under the careful attention of his roommate, Isaac recovered.

"What has happened to me?" Isaac asked. He had awaken at the regular time. His mind was refreshed and clear.

John Wickins said, "For two weeks you had gone without proper rest, without sleep, without exercise or regular food. You had lectures to attend in the day, study in the evening, and the comet at night. It was too much."

Although Isaac had not solved the comet problem, he did learn an important lesson: The human body could only be pushed so far, no matter what the desire driving it. Rest and exercise were necessary for good health.

He learned to exercise while studying; he stood up while writing notes. He walked around the room while thinking. John Wickins saw to it that he and Isaac played a game of tennis once or twice each week.

Isaac Newton and twenty-five other students received their Bachelor of Arts degrees from Trinity in 1665. Except for Doctor Barrow, none of the other professors looked upon him as an outstanding student.

But Doctor Barrow spoke up for his pupil. "God has planted an unusually productive mind in this young man. It is our duty to clear the stone from around it so that the plant may grow tall and strong."

What should Isaac do now? Return to the farm? Marry Catherine and settle down as a country preacher? Stay on at Trinity and work for his Master's degree?

Sixty miles away in London the decision was taken out of his hands. The Black Death struck. It spread across England. On August 8, 1665, the University closed its doors. Students scattered to the countryside.

CHAPTER SEVEN:

London: Death and Fire

Children were singing:
> *Ring a ring o' roses,*
> *A pocket full of posies.*
> *Ashes to ashes,*
> *We all fall down!*

But this was a grim sort of nursery rhyme. This rhyme told of the Black Death, the most feared plague to strike European cities.

The "ring a ring o' roses" talked about in the rhyme was a sure sign of the disease; a bright red ring circled a black spot on the victim's skin. Some people in a desperate attempt to ward off the dreaded disease stuffed their pockets with posies, but this remedy had no value. The victim's skin turned the color of ashes and death struck him down, sometimes within twenty-four hours.

At first, the plague had been confined to London, but then it spread to Cambridge.

John Wickins brought the dreadful news. "The Black Death has come to Trinity. A man fell dead yesterday. His body carried the mark."

Isaac Newton looked up from a sketch he was drawing. Alarm crossed his face. "Will it spread to Woolsthorpe?"

"No, not to the country," John Wickins said. "For some reason the Black Death only strikes in crowded cities and university towns. Ten thousand people have died in London and it is getting worse. Some say it is due to bad air, others think it is caused by overcrowding. The college must dismiss so we can escape."

Trinity did close during August of 1665. The students scattered to the countryside. No one knew how to fight the disease. Nearly everyone fled when a city was struck by the plague. Often no one remained behind to bury the dead. Entire towns became ghost towns.

Friendly people changed; they became suspicious of strangers. One church leader said, "Shut your doors against your friends, and if a man passeth over the fields avoid him as you would in time of war."

Isaac packed to leave Trinity. Doctor Barrow came to see him off. Although Doctor Barrow taught mathematics full time, he still considered himself a preacher of the Gospel. He planned upon using his free time for missionary work.

Doctor Barrow said, "I am afraid many students and teachers do not know what to do with this forced vacation."

"So am I," Isaac admitted.

Doctor Barrow said, "This paper you presented to me in which you explain your discovery of the binomial theorem is an outstanding bit of mathematical work. I mailed it to Doctor Wallis. He assures me it is the work of a first class mathematician."

Isaac smiled, "Mathematicians are not in much demand at the moment."

"True," Doctor Barrow said. "But if you use your vacation wisely, I would work to find you a position at Trinity as a Fellow when the classes resume."

Isaac said farewell to John Wickins and Doctor Barrow and returned to his mother's farm where he set up a small writing desk and table in the apple orchard. For more than eighteen months he enjoyed leisure time and quiet surroundings. He began to think deeply about the problems his teachers had mentioned during classes.

"How long will you be with us?" his mother asked.

"Until the plague runs its course," Isaac said. "Some believe it will die out during cold weather. Others say we will be out for two years. I will help with the farm."

"No!" his mother cried. "Mary and Hannah and Benjamin are old enough for the chores. You are a scholar now. Rest and study."

The orchard was a wonderful place for thinking during the summer. It was bright with color, filled with the smell of growing things from the nearby garden. Red apples hung overhead within reach.

Isaac took notes constantly, putting down his thoughts in an organized way. He began a study of the Bible, especially the prophecies of Daniel in the Old Testament.

Isaac read about Daniel:

Children in whom was no blemish, but well favoured, and skilful in all wisdom, and cunning in knowledge, and understanding science . . . (Daniel 1:4).

In many ways, Isaac saw a reflection of his own life in the life of Daniel. The young prince had been trained in science, but he never lost his devotion to God.

Isaac had the training to be a good Bible scholar. He knew Latin, Greek, and Hebrew. He began a manuscript in which he gave his reasons for believing two verses in the New Testament had been translated incorrectly in the King James Translation.

Mary Smith, his older half sister, often helped with construction projects in the kitchen. At other times she fixed a tray of food and brought it to the orchard.

Her half brother, she decided, was too thin.
But his brown eyes and square jaw gave his face
a determined look, and his hair turning white
made him look older. Maybe he was not handsome because of his long nose, but his face showed
an iron strength of will. But he seldom smiled.

"You're too serious," Mary said. She watched
as he divided out a division problem.

"I am testing my binomial theorem."

"What is a theorem?"

Isaac explained, "A theorem is a rule. With the
binomial theorem I can rewrite a hard problem as
a long line of simpler ones. Lately, I have been
trying to use it to work more difficult problems—"
His voice trailed off as he continued his calculations, lost in thought.

Isaac had developed a way of using his binomial theorem to add together an infinite number
of very small numbers. He called it *fluxions* from
a Latin word which means "to flow." The "flow-
ing" math allowed him to find the areas enclosed
by curves which constantly changed direction.

Mathematicians could find the area of simple
figures such as squares and triangles. But it was
more difficult for circles and ellipses and impossible for figures such as hyperbolas and parabolas.

Someday, when he grew more skilled in the
use of fluxions, he felt confident he could figure
the orbits of comets, but for now he had to con-
tent himself with figuring the areas of earthbound
objects.

Isaac mounted a horse and rode to an ancient
Norman manor house at Boothby. The manor
was famous for its great curving archways. Isaac
measured the archways. He used his fluxions to
find the area enclosed by the archways. He carried out his computations to fifty-two places to
check the accuracy.

"I am ashamed to tell how many places of figures I carried these computations, having no other business at the time," Isaac wrote in a letter to Doctor Barrow. "Here is a short paper explaining my methods. As you can see it goes farther than the work of Wallis and Descartes."

When he tired of one study, he switched to something else: mathematics, theology, Bible history, optics, telescopes or gravity. *Gravity.* Now that was a problem!

He first learned about what others thought about gravity in a book *The Discovery of the New World in the Moon* by John Wilkins. He was the writer of *Mathematicall Magick,* another book Isaac had enjoyed. John Wilkins's books were noted for their wild speculations on one hand and solid descriptions of facts on the other.

Gravity, whatever it was, held the planets to the sun and the moon to the earth.

Kepler, like the ancient Greeks, incorrectly believed a moving object such as a ball rolling across a table would stop unless a force "pushed" it along. No, said Galileo. The ball would keep going in a straight line as long as no outside force slowed it. The rolling ball stopped because of friction between it and the table.

The moon, like a ball on a perfectly smooth table, kept moving year after year without slowing down. But the moon did not travel in a straight line. Instead, it circled the earth.

What caused its path to bend into a circle? No one had a good reason.

Then one day an apple fell from the tree overhead and banged on Newton's work table in the orchard. Later Newton mentioned this in a letter to a friend. He picked up the apple, and as he held it, he noticed the half-moon which had risen in the east.

He had an inspiration. The moon didn't fly out into space because it, like the apple, was held in place by the pull of the earth's gravity.

The moon and apple were both subject to the same force of gravity.

Learned men up to this time had never thought it possible for the motions of earthly things to be compared to the motions of heavenly bodies. "The motions of heavenly bodies do not follow the laws of earth," they said.

Newton believed otherwise. "Providence puts everything in order, both on earth and in the heavens."

He thought, "The moon is sixty times further from the center of the earth as the apple. Will the force of gravity be sixty times as weak?"

To his surprise, his calculations showed the force to be weaker not by sixty times but by sixty times sixty. Gravity grew weaker by the square of the distance.

Isaac wrote a letter to Doctor Barrow. "I compared the force necessary to keep the moon in her orbit with the force of gravity at the surface of the earth, and found them to agree pretty nearly to the inverse square law that I worked out."

Newton tore up the letter. *Pretty nearly*. That was not closely enough! Science was no place for half-finished ideas.

During December of 1665 the cold weather caused a temporary halt to the Black Death. Isaac visited Trinity College for a few weeks. He asked about going to London to buy optical glass to make a telescope.

Doctor Barrow did not think much of that idea. "Parts of the city are deserted. A hundred thousand Londoners have died and many of the rest have fled."

Isaac returned to Woolsthorpe. Nine months passed. The Black Death returned to take its terrible toll. Then in September of 1666, Uncle William arrived with news of a disaster. "London is afire! It has been burning for three days."

A few weeks later a letter from his roommate spelled out the disaster. "It is the worse fire in London's history, three-fourths of the city is in ruins. The fire began in the house of the king's baker on Pudding Street near London Bridge. While the city burned, people huddled in boats on the Thames River. The fire has burned itself out after destroying ten thousand homes. Gresham College is still standing. City leaders are meeting there to plan a new city. . . ."

Isaac looked up from the letter. "Gresham College is Doctor Barrow's old school."

The letter continued, "Christopher Wren is in charge of building the city back. He intends to put in wide streets, build homes of brick instead of wood. He has promised more churches and hospitals. He thinks more canals for better drainage will eliminate the danger of the Black Death returning."

After the fire ended the people of London waited for the return of the Black Death. But it didn't come. By spring of 1667 the word was out. Trinity would reopen March 25, the first day of Easter Term.

CHAPTER EIGHT:

Nest Among the Stars

Doctor Barrow welcomed Isaac back to Trinity with a firm handshake and pleased smile. "Well, tell me about your discoveries."

Isaac gave a little smile. "I did a few experiments with light and wrote a paper about fluxions which may someday amount to something. That is all. The work is not finished. I must lay it aside now to study for a Fellowship"

Doctor Barrow said, "You will succeed. I have faith in your ability."

Isaac spoke freely to Doctor Barrow. "The professors expect Fellowship contestants to know all about the classics. I am not certain of success as you are."

Doctor Barrow said, "Your chances have improved during the vacation. This year nine positions must be filled."

"Why so many?" Isaac asked.

"Eighteen months have passed since the last selections," Doctor Barrow said. "There are more unfilled teaching positions than usual."

Isaac went to his room. John Wickins had arrived before him. His roommate gave another—and more grisly—reason for the large number of vacant

Fellowships. "On two separate times professors died from falls down the stairs."

"Two! Surely the stairs are not that dangerous."

John Wickins said, "The professors were tangle-footed."

"Too much drink?" Isaac asked.

John Wickins nodded soberly. "They broke their necks after drinking too much. Such disgraceful conduct is all too common. The Master of Trinity should put an end to it. But Doctor Ferne was too weak, and his successor is just as bad."

The Fellowship Committee interviewed Isaac. They made their decision. He was accepted.

Isaac Newton, Fellow of Trinity College! The title gave him free room and board and a garden plot near the main gate. Best of all the garden had a small brick building. He could make it into a chemistry laboratory. Some experiments were too dangerous to carry out in his chambers.

Not only was he getting what he wanted, but he was being paid as well!

John Wickins congratulated him. "You will receive a salary?"

"Yes, one hundred pounds—more than I've ever had before. My mother has made special sacrifices to allow me to come to Trinity. All that is over. I have money and time to do the research I have longed to do.

"One other thing," Isaac said. "Fellows of Trinity are entitled to a private room."

John Wickins showed his disappointment. "I will have to break in a new roommate. Must you move?"

Isaac looked happy. "I was hoping you would invite me to remain."

John Wickins kidded him, "You would starve without me to remind you to eat. What will you study this term?"

"Doctor Barrow has asked me to help him write a book on optics. I will study the nature of light and color."

On rainy days Isaac rushed outside to look for a rainbow. On frosty nights he stayed up to measure the halo around the moon.

One day John Wickins walked across the campus and saw a curious sight: Isaac Newton was sitting on a stool in the garden and blowing soap bubbles.

Isaac held a clay pipe. He had filled the pipe, not with tobacco, but with soapy water. Bubbles floated in the air around him. Isaac peered at the bubbles in deep concentration.

John wondered if Isaac had taken leave of his senses.

Isaac called to his roommate. "Watch. See the colors that shine on the surface of the bubbles. At first all of the colors are there—red and green and blue. Then, just before the bubbles burst, the colors vanish."

"Why?" John Wickins asked.

Isaac said, "The thickness of the soap film has something to do with it, but I don't completely know the reason."

Even Isaac had grown weary of reading the many conflicting theories about light and color. The books contained no facts. Isaac thought to himself, "A single experiment carried out carefully is worth a dozen books filled with guesses. Go straight to the problem!"

Isaac bought a prism at nearby Stourbridge Fair. Sunlight flashing through the triangular piece of glass threw out a vivid rainbow. The colors ran from red through orange, yellow, green, blue, indigo to violet. Isaac called the rainbow formed by a prism a *spectrum*.

He covered the window of his chamber with a shutter and let in a tiny beam of sunlight.

"Look at this," Isaac said. "When I put the prism near the opening, the spectrum is cast on the far wall."

John Wickins drew in his breath. He marveled at the intense colors splashed across the white paper. "Beautiful!"

Isaac said, "According to all that I have read the middle of the spectrum should be white."

John Wickins looked closer. "But the middle is green."

Isaac said, "For centuries natural philosophers have argued about the nature of sunlight. Aristotle said sunlight was perfect and pure. It contains no color he said."

Isaac reversed a second prism and placed it in the path of the spectrum. "Look. The colors come back together into a beam of white light. This simple experiment shows sunlight can be made by mixing the colors together. Aristotle was wrong!"

Isaac continued his simple, but careful, experiments. He saw that a telescope lens acted like a weak prism. It split starlight into the colors. This explained the ring of color which circled bright objects in the first telescope he made.

Could the unwanted color be removed? Isaac set up a frame that held red, green, and blue threads. He looked at the threads through a telescope. He could not focus on all three colors at the same time no matter how he tried.

A lens telescope would always have the color problem he decided. Very well, if a lens would not work, a mirror would. A mirror reflects all colors the same amount. Isaac decided to use a curving mirror with a shallow surface shaped like a saucer.

Isaac talked about it with Doctor Barrow. "About ten years ago James Gregory in Scotland designed a perfectly good mirror telescope. His design called for a metal mirror made of highly reflective alloy of copper and tin. At the top of the tube was a second mirror. The second mirror is small and curved. The second mirror sends the light back down the tube. The observer views the image through a hole in the middle of the main mirror."

Doctor Barrow said, "I am aware of his design. But when he took it to professional lens grinders, they failed to make one. They saw the hole in the middle of the main mirror and shook their heads. It can't be done."

Isaac unfolded a sketch of a short, stubby telescope. "Here is my idea. Replace the little mirror with a flat one. Instead of sending the light down the tube, tilt the flat mirror and reflect the light to one side through a hole in the tube. This gets around the hole in the main mirror."

"Who will make it for you?" Doctor Barrow asked.

"I will make it myself," Isaac said. "If I waited for other people to make things for me, I would never get anything done."

He needed a furnace to melt metal for the mirror. Isaac laid bricks to build a fireproof furnace in the garden workshop. Students smiled as they passed. A Fellow laying bricks did not fit Trinity traditions.

What others thought of him did not bother Isaac. "I delight in working with my hands. The mind grows tired when not balanced by honest labor with the hands."

The alloy for the main mirror had to polish to a bright, shiny surface. Many experiments failed before Isaac hit upon a proper blend of metals. It was hot, dangerous work. He wrote a paper describing his methods:

"I first melted the copper alone, then put in some arsenic which being melted I stirred them a little together, bewaring in the meantime that I

draw not in breath near the fumes. After that I
put in the tin, and again, so soon as that was
melted, which was very suddenly, I stirred them
well together and immediately poured them off."

Until then astronomers used long, clumsy telescopes that shook in the wind and warped in
damp weather.

Newton finished his telescope in 1668. Soon everyone at Trinity was talking about it.

"Only six inches long!" one student said.

"The tube is no larger than a copper coin!" another student marveled.

Isaac's "toy" worked better than other telescopes six feet long.

It had a magnification of forty power and could
be carried in one hand. He made the entire telescope by hand—tube, mirror, mounting, eyepiece
—everything! It gave a rock steady view, even
when the wind blew. Yet it could be pointed to
any part of the sky.

At night he set up his tiny telescope on a table
in the garden. Students and teachers gathered to
look at the inky black craters of the moon, the
dazzling white "horns" of Venus, and the four
moons circling around Jupiter.

"Clear and sharp," Doctor Barrow said. "The
colors are in their proper places."

The wonder of the night sky excited the imagi-
nation. Isaac knew the Bible said it best: "The
heavens declare the glory of God; and the firma-
ment sheweth his handywork" (Psalm 19:1 King
James Translation).

The telescope was not the only thing which interested Isaac during his first year as a Fellow. He
worked on other matters, both scientific and religious.

He grew fresh vegetables in the garden, filled
the chemistry shed with flasks and retorts, and

filled his room with all sorts of inventions. He made a burning glass, tested a new thermometer, and built an ear trumpet to help the hard of hearing.

His thoughts were never far from the Bible. He made an important discovery. The Bible could be used to trace the history of ancient countries. He spent many hours studying old writings and Biblical manuscripts to work out the history of Egypt. Isaac found that the Bible contains true history.

Doctor Barrow considered the work so important he opened his private library to Isaac.

"Telling others of new ideas is a real problem," Doctor Barrow said. "The Royal Society is one answer. Each month men of learning meet together and exchange ideas. Another idea is to exchange letters. John Collins has a sort of clearinghouse in London. He copies important lectures and mails them throughout the scientific world. I believe your notes on the fluxions should be sent to him."

Isaac said, "Send the paper, but leave off my name."

"What! Most scholars desire fame. They sign their names to everything, even shopping lists. Your paper is outstanding."

Isaac, however, feared fame would interfere with his studies.

Within a month John Collins reported back that other mathematicians had demanded the name of the writer of the paper.

"You must allow your name to be put on the manuscript," Doctor Barrow told Isaac.

"Very well," Isaac agreed reluctantly.

Doctor Barrow wrote to John Collins. "I am glad my friend's paper has given so much satisfaction. The name of the author is Isaac Newton, a Fellow of the College, and a young man who is only in his second year since he took the degree of Master of Arts. He has made very great progress in this branch of mathematics."

Doctor Barrow believed Isaac should be better known. "Pack the telescope," Doctor Barrow said. "I want to show it to the Royal Society."

Doctor Barrow took the telescope to London. He showed it before the Royal Society.

Isaac waited for his return. He wondered what kind of reception the telescope would get.

Doctor Barrow came back. He beamed a smile. "They were amazed," he reported. "King Charles came to look through it. Christopher Wren was impressed. He is still directing the rebuilding of London after the fire. Even bad-tempered Robert Hooke admitted it was an efficient instrument.

"They crowded around like children around a Christmas surprise. I told them you had the hands of a carpenter and the head of a mathematician."

A few days later a letter arrived from Henry Oldenburg, Secretary of the Royal Society. He praised the instrument. "Your telescope caused quite a stir."

Isaac read the letter. "I am surprised to see so much interest in an invention on which I have put so little value."

"Your reputation has soared," Doctor Barrow said.

Isaac stood by the window and looked out over the campus. "The excitement has stunned me. Never before did I think it might be possible that I had any ability above that of the common student."

"But you must accept that fact," Doctor Barrow said.

"I simply think about the problem until little by little it dawns into a full and clear light," Isaac

said.

Doctor Barrow used the success of Isaac's telescope to make a special announcement. "I am resigning my position to devote full time to the study of Scripture. I will step down as Lucasian Professor."

Isaac could not imagine Trinity without Doctor Barrow. "Who could take your place?"

Doctor Barrow said, "I have already chosen a successor. You—Isaac Newton—will fill the position!"

Isaac stood speechless.

Doctor Barrow continued, "For me it is a great method to fulfill my desire to work in the ministry. At the same time I will be certain the mathematics chair is filled with a person able to perform the duties."

The teaching position was one of the most famous "chairs" in the scientific world. Isaac took the job at the age of twenty-seven. It was a very early age to take such an important post.

His salary doubled. Isaac watched his heart. He must not put money or fame before God. When things troubled him, he wrote prayers to God. He took pen and wrote, "Set my heart on Thee. Turn me away from money and pleasure."

The new post brought sad news as well. Trinity professors could not marry. He and Catherine would have to call off their engagement.

He would miss her. Catherine made him happy whenever he was around her. Yes, he would miss her greatly.

Until then he had looked upon every vacation as a chance to rush back to Lincolnshire to see her. This Christmas he didn't look forward to the difficult duty of telling her the bad news.

His mother told him, "She knows. Ralf Clark has explained it to her. She understands."

When they met Catherine smiled to him through trembling lips. She said, "I knew this was coming ever since the plague year. You talked to me with a faraway look in your eyes. Any woman could tell."

"I'm sorry," Isaac said.

Catherine said, "Hawks must sometimes fly alone. I will pray for you. We will always be friends. Have a safe journey back to Trinity."

"God be with you," Isaac said.

Several months later Hannah Smith wrote to her son. "Catherine Storey married the Vincent boy. Remember to send the newlyweds a gift."

His eyes turned misty. A lump filled his throat. Isaac felt terribly alone. At age twenty-seven all his ties at Woolsthorpe were broken. Trinity College was his new home.

CHAPTER NINE:

The Invisible College

During December of 1671 exciting news reached Trinity. Doctor Ward, the Bishop of Salisbury, put forth Isaac's name for membership in the Royal Society. On January 11, 1672, the Royal Society voted. They elected Isaac as a member.

At the Royal Society each Wednesday the finest thinkers in the world met in London to talk about new discoveries. Doctor Barrow was a member. So was Isaac's letter-writing friend John Collins. Other members included Samuel Pepys of the Royal Navy; Charles Montague, the politician; John Locke, the physician; and Robert Boyle, who was famous for his chemical studies.

Doctor Barrow climbed the steps to Isaac's room and congratulated him. "The Royal Society is filled with remarkable people. They refuse to accept the ancient Greeks as the only source of knowledge. *Nothing by mere authority*, that's the Society's motto."

"Do you know Robert Boyle?" Isaac asked.

"Yes," Doctor Barrow said. "He is tall and slender with a calm voice. When I visited at his

home, the rooms were filled with glasses and pots and chemical instruments. Books overflowed from shelves and bundles of paper tumbled from the desk. There was barely room for us to sit. He is writing another book about his experiments with air."

"Which of his books should I read?" Isaac asked.

Doctor Barrow laughed. "All of them!"

When Doctor Barrow left, Isaac walked to Trinity library. He checked out *A History of the Royal Society*. In the early 1650s Robert Boyle began meeting with young scholars who let experiments, not guesses, guide them. They bypassed the stiff, old-fashioned method of learning.

Robert Boyle called the group the Invisible College. At this time about fifty people belonged to the Invisible College. They attended Wednesday meetings at Gresham College off and on.

One of the members of the Invisible College was Samuel Pepys. Although Samuel Pepys did not claim to be a scientist, he worked at the Navy department and enjoyed meeting with the young scholars.

Robert Boyle talked to Samuel Pepys. "Many useful ideas lay forgotten because of poor communication between scientists and inventors. The Invisible College should be open for others to join."

"We will need a Royal Charter," said Samuel Pepys. "I will speak to King Charles."

In 1663 King Charles II officially recognized the Invisible College under a new name: *The Royal Society of London for the Promotion of Natural History.*

Isaac Newton believed Robert Boyle would be an interesting person to meet. He said to John Wickins, "Robert Boyle is concerned with showing that science and religion are not in conflict. In fact they work together. Science shows that there is a purpose behind the grand design of the universe."

Isaac lectured to students now. He talked about light. He spoke only about things which he had proven true by experiments. "I want no part of reckless speculation with no regard to facts."

Isaac had keen senses that matched his skill as an observer. One morning he announced to those at breakfast, "The Dutch fleet and the English fleet have engaged in a sea battle. The English ships are in retreat toward our shores."

Those who heard him were puzzled. "How can you be so certain? Information takes hours to reach London, and a day for the news to come to us."

"Nevertheless," Isaac insisted, "the battle is this very moment taking place."

"Explain yourself!" they cried.

"Very well. Early this morning I awoke early and went for a walk in the still night air. I heard the boom of ship's cannons. With the passage of an hour the sound grew louder. The battle is moving closer. English ships are retreating!"

"You heard the cannons?" They were amazed. "The Channel is sixty miles away!"

Isaac said, "Night sounds carry easily."

The wars finally sputtered to an end after both sides suffered a series of defeats.

Isaac's sense of touch was exceptionally well developed. He could work with tiny tools; he could "weigh" an object just by hefting it with his hands.

Isaac decided to show his gratitude to the Royal Society for electing him a member. "I will make a telescope and give it to them," he said to John Wickins. "At the same time I can write a paper telling them of my endeavors with light."

The second mirror telescope pleased Isaac. It turned out to be better than the first. He shipped it to the Royal Society. At the same time he wrote a paper. The paper told of his prism experiments. He called the paper *The Composition of White Light*.

Doctor Barrow had become the chaplain to King Charles. He traveled throughout England. People came to listen to his sermons. He was the best preacher in England, or so the King said.

Often Doctor Barrow visited Trinity, spoke in chapel, and then talked with Isaac about events in London.

Doctor Barrow said, "The Royal Society greatly appreciated the telescope."

"What of the paper on light and color?" Isaac asked.

Doctor Barrow smiled ruefully. "Well, they appointed a committee to report on your paper."

"What does that mean?" Isaac wondered.

"Some scientists think you are too young to put forth theories of your own. Especially when you disagree with them."

"But the paper is not filled with theories! It contains the observations I made with the prism.

Surely that cannot be put aside."

"Your paper will be printed. In fact, the order is at the printer. And the Royal Society has published an order which thanks you for your very ingenious discourse. Well-known scientists all over the world will soon be reading your paper. Christian Huygens in Holland will certainly have something to say."

Isaac said, "He is an experienced telescope maker."

"Yes, but he makes lens telescopes, not mirror ones. He will look upon your mirror telescope as a competitor of his. A committee has been formed to reply to your paper. They will put their objections in a report."

"Report?" Isaac asked. He was startled by the news.

Doctor Barrow said, "Surely you do not expect your theories to be accepted without question."

"My paper contains facts, not untested theories. Who can object to facts based upon careful observations?"

Doctor Barrow clasped Isaac by the shoulder. He leaned forward. "Robert Hooke heads the committee. He will disagree with you."

"Why?" Isaac asked.

"Hooke disagrees with everyone!" Barrow said. Hooke seems to enjoy starting bitter quarrels."

"Tell me more about him," Isaac said.

Doctor Barrow described Hooke. "His figure is frail and badly crippled. His limbs are shrunken. His hair hangs in uncombed locks over a face twisted by constant headaches and pain. His temper cannot be predicted. He seldom sleeps, probably because of pain and a restless mind. He is constantly active and only takes short naps during the day."

"What of his work in science?" Isaac asked.

"He is a genius. No one doubts that. The Royal Society employs Hooke to show three or four experiments at each weekly meeting. During the past ten years he has demonstrated more than fifteen hundred experiments. He claims to be an expert in many fields."

Isaac said, "I have read his *Micrographia*. The book certainly shows that he understands the principles of a microscope. His drawings of snow-flakes and feathers and fleas are wonderful in their detail."

Doctor Barrow smiled. "Some say the fleas for his study came from his own body."

Isaac was anxious for the committee to enter its report. Finally the report did arrive. Hooke had written it.

Isaac read it. He was stunned. "It is worse than I feared."

Hooke agreed that the mirror telescope worked. But he more or less told Isaac to let experienced scientists explain why it worked.

Hooke said, "I have read the paper of Mr. Newton about color. It is a nice little paper. But as for his explanation for color, I cannot see yet any undeniable argument to convince me of the certainty thereof." Like most scientists, Hooke still believed the prism created the colors and that white light was pure.

Isaac carefully wrote a full reply. He answered each of Hooke's objections. "Mr. Hooke thinks it is his business to find fault with me. But he knows well it is not for one man to set down rules to the studies of another, especially when he does not understand the grounds on which he proceeds."

Time and again he cried out for those who doubted to try the experiments themselves. He wrote: "You know, the proper method of looking

into the properties of things is to deduce them from experiments. If the experiments which I urge are defective, it cannot be difficult to show the defects. But I am certain of my claims."

Huygens in Holland and Pardies in Paris joined with Hooke in ripping apart Newton's paper.

At first Isaac answered each letter. But as the months passed he saw that many men talked about the experimental method, but few followed it.

Isaac put down his pen. His arm and fingers were stiff from writing. Isaac said to his roommate, "They speak as if facts are an unnecessary bother."

Isaac paced the floor. He said, "Surely any honest scholar would realize truths cannot be discovered by arguing with others. Science begins with experiments. There can be no argument against facts and experiments."

John Wickins did not agree. "Seldom are new ideas welcome, even by men who should know better."

"What am I going to do?" Isaac pleaded. "My equipment lays untouched. My lectures suffer. My time is spent with pen in hand writing letters which are never read. It must end!"

Doctor Barrow tried to help Isaac through the difficult time. He said, "Hooke is not like you. He does not spend much time with any one thing. Each week he must come up with new and interesting experiments for the Royal Society. One day he throws himself into the study of snowflakes. By afternoon he is sketching an idea for a flying machine. The next morning he is building an improved microscope. He looks into many things, but he perfects little."

"But what of his latest claim? He says he invented my mirror telescope first."

Barrow shrugged. "He often claims the inventions of others. No one will believe him."

Isaac shook his head sadly. "Science is not a battleground for petty quarrels. I have asked Secretary Oldenburg to read my letters and mark out anything that might cause harm."

"How do you intend to answer this last charge?" Doctor Barrow asked. He pointed to a letter from Huygens.

Isaac said, "I will not answer it. I became Lucasian Professor of Mathematics because the position would give me time to think and experiment. It is a bother to write letters to blind men who refuse to even carry out the experiments."

Isaac decided to resign from the Royal Society as well. He wrote Henry Oldenburg. "Remove my name from the Royal Society. It has caused nothing but trouble. I see a man must either be resolved to put out nothing new, or to become a slave to defend it."

Henry Oldenburg, a Puritan who dressed in the traditional clothes of black and white, was a German by birth, but educated at Oxford. When he read Isaac's letter of resignation, he refused to accept it. He talked over the matter with Robert Boyle. "Isaac is too valuable a scientist for the Society to lose because of petty bickering. I will pay his Society dues myself."

Slowly the debate died down. As the years passed more and more scientists began to agree with Newton's views upon color and light.

Isaac learned another important lesson. Even men who are supposed to be dedicated to truth can become blinded by their own pet ideas.

CHAPTER TEN:

A Problem of Conscience

Isaac Newton became Trinity's best-known teacher. A legend grew up about his absent-minded ways. When a problem caught his fancy, he put aside everything else.

For days he would not show up in the Common Hall for meals. A Sizar brought a tray of food to his chambers. The Sizar returned for the tray. "He didn't touch the food. Look, the food is dried out and cold."

Another student said "Professor Newton is absent-minded all right. Have you heard about the time someone stopped him in the court when he was on the way for supper? When they finished talking, Professor Newton walked back to his chambers. He completely forgot that he had not eaten."

The Sizar said, "He doesn't act like a professor. He awakes each morning and walks about in his garden. It is an eerie sight to see him walking across the campus on a foggy morning. His black gown flaps behind him. His hands are stained with ink. His clothes have holes burned in them by acid."

"Have you attended any of his lectures?"

"Not often. They are above my head. Once, he came to the lecture hall and I was the only student there. He delivered his lecture with as much satisfaction as if the hall had been filled. With or without an audience he delivers his lectures!"

"Well," the other student said, "at least the lectures are not lost. The library considers them important enough to keep a copy of them."

Isaac lectured only once a week. This gave him plenty of time to experiment, read and write up the lectures. Two days a week students could come to him for help with their studies. For some reason, his help sessions were much more useful than his lectures.

One day in 1673 John Wickins received a letter. "Isaac, this is the assignment I have been waiting to receive."

"You have a vicarage!" Isaac guessed.

"Yes," John Wickins said. "I will pastor the church at Stoke Edith near Monmouth."

Isaac was happy for his roommate, but sad to see him depart. The room would not be the same with John Wickins gone. "Now is the time for me to move to new quarters," Isaac decided.

Isaac moved into a two-room suite in the north-east corner of the Great Court. One of the rooms he changed into a chemistry laboratory. At the head of the stairs in a window he mounted one of his mirror telescopes. His Sizar had a room nearby.

The time came to say good-bye to John Wickins. "I am happy for you," Isaac said. "Preaching the Word of God is an important calling."

"You have been a wonderful friend," John Wickins said.

"It is you who has been wonderful. Who else would endure stains on the floor from my chemical studies, unpleasant smells in the air, and strange hours. I am sorry to see you leave."

John Wickins said, "At least Doctor Barrow is returning to Trinity. It is time the College had a strong Master."

Trinity had a new Master! King Charles II appointed Doctor Barrow the Master of Trinity. Doctor Barrow returned to Cambridge in 1673.

Isaac welcomed Doctor Barrow. "Everyone is happy to see you return. But no one rejoices more than I do!"

Doctor Barrow looked over his former student. Isaac had a thoughtful forehead, square chin, and piercing eyes which grew intent when he was thinking upon a difficult problem.

"I intend to enforce the rules," Doctor Barrow said. "It will be a difficult job. Too many Fellows take advantage of their position and stay on at Trinity. They neither teach nor earn their keep by doing real study."

Several months passed. Doctor Barrow enforced all the rules under which the College had been chartered. One of the rules, however, directly concerned Isaac Newton.

"A Fellowship is for seven years," Doctor Barrow said. "At the end of that time a Fellow is expected to complete his religious training and be ordained as a minister."

"But I am a teacher, not a student," Isaac said.

"That is true," Doctor Barrow said. "But for a Fellow to remain at Trinity, he must take Holy Orders."

"I cannot take Holy Orders, Doctor Barrow," Isaac said.

Barrow said, "I know you are a deeply religious man. But can you explain yourself?"

Isaac was not very good in explaining himself to others. He tried to tell Doctor Barrow why he could not take Holy Orders and why he could not become a member of the Church of England as an ordained preacher.

Isaac said, "I have a fundamental belief in the Bible as the Word of God, written by men who were inspired. I study the Bible daily—"

"Yes," Doctor Barrow said. "You know more about the Bible than all the others at Trinity put together. But why can you not take Holy Orders?"

Isaac said, "We are to acknowledge one God, the Creator of all things. God is the same God, always and everywhere. He is able to revive the dead. He has revived Jesus Christ, our Redeemer, who has gone into the heavens to receive a kingdom and prepare a place for us."

Isaac continued, "The Bible tells us to 'Prove all things, hold fast that which is true.' The Church of England has thirty-nine articles of faith. I believe some of the articles are in error. I simply could not take Holy Orders because I would be pledging to uphold rules which I think are wrong. Some of the duties which I would be called upon to do would be in conflict with my beliefs about the New Testament."

Isaac did not like the way human traditions had changed the Church at Trinity. It was no longer like the Church which he read about in the New Testament. He wished to worship God in his own way.

Doctor Barrow said, "It would be to your advantage to take Holy Orders and become a clergyman. But I understand. You must worship God in the way you think is right."

Isaac said, "I believe I can serve God better by not being formally bound to the Church of England."

Religion was not a part-time hobby for Isaac. He studied every Biblical manuscript he could lay his hand upon. He had more than twelve different Bibles. He wrote many pages about the Bible and other religious matters.

He wanted freedom in religious matters. He remembered the Civil War when a person's religion was not a personal matter. Religion became the reason for war.

But—Isaac couldn't accept the thought of leaving Trinity. "After all, I do teach here. It isn't the same as those who hold a Fellowship and do not teach classes."

Doctor Barrow said, "I see your point, but the rule must be enforced."

"Surely something can be done," Isaac said.

Doctor Barrow grew thoughtful for a moment. "There is one hope. I waited to mention this because the chances for success are very remote."

"Well?" Isaac asked.

"Write a petition to King Charles. He has the power to grant you permission to stay on as Lucasian Professor."

"I will write the petition in my own hand," Isaac said. Although he did not like the idea of asking for favors from politicians, he did want to stay on at Trinity.

Doctor Barrow said, "We will enlist the aid of the Royal Society in London. The Society members will help. You will be called to London for the hearing. Plan upon staying several weeks. Court matters move slowly."

Early in February 1675, Isaac caught the coach for London. He rented a room and stayed in London for six weeks. Each morning he arose and made the rounds. He visited with important people who could help his cause.

To his surprise well-known people received him

with pleasure. They pledged their support. Isaac talked with England's greatest men.

Isaac visited Robert Boyle in his house in Pall Mall. The two men spent most of their time in Boyle's chemistry laboratory.

Robert Boyle told Isaac about Francis Aston. "A few months ago he asked for a similar dispensation from King Charles."

"Was it granted?" Isaac asked.

"No," Robert Boyle said. "Sir Joseph Williamson, Secretary of State, backed his cause. But King Charles turned down his request."

"Then my case has little chance of succeeding," Isaac said.

"Don't be discouraged. John Locke and Samuel Pepys are on your side of this matter."

John Locke had said, "Mr. Newton is a very valuable man, not only for his wonderful skill in mathematics, but in divinity too, and his great knowledge of the Scriptures, wherein I know few his equal."

One good thing did come because of the petition. Isaac attended his first meeting of the Royal Society. On February 18, Henry Oldenburg introduced Isaac to the Royal Society. "You may be satisfied that the members in general esteem and love you," he assured Isaac.

After the meeting the men pressed forward to greet him. Henry Oldenburg, the solid German; Samuel Pepys, the Naval Secretary; Robert Boyle, England's greatest chemist; even Hooke welcomed Isaac. They were very friendly!

Christopher Wren was a popular leader in the Society. He had begun as an astronomer at Oxford. There he studied comets and the rings of Saturn. At age thirty he took up architecture— the design and construction of buildings. He went to Europe during the Black Death. When the

Great Fire destroyed London, he came forward with a grand design to rebuild the city.

Wren said, "We have designed fifty new parish churches. They are finished. But the work on St. Paul's has only begun."

Isaac said, "I have heard about your model for St. Paul's Protestant Church."

"Come with me," Wren suggested. "Let me show you the model. The Great Fire damaged the old church building beyond repair. It will be pulled down and a new building put up."

Wren's model impressed Isaac. "The design is like nothing I've seen!" he said.

Wren said, "It is growing dark. We had best return to your quarters. The streets are not safe at night. Too many criminals are about."

On March 12, 1675, His Majesty Charles II handed down his decision. He granted the petition! Isaac could retain his Trinity professorship. He would not have to take Holy Orders. The order stood as long as Isaac held the Lucasian Chair and taught classes.

Isaac said good-bye to Henry Oldenburg. "My visit to London has renewed my faith in my fellow scientists. Many of the members of the Royal Society disagreed with me about the nature of light and color. But they instantly came forward to offer help."

"It goes both ways," said Oldenburg. "Many people were mistaken about you. They only knew you by your letters. They thought you were arrogant and quick tempered. But in person they saw you in a different light. You are considerate and friendly. And charming, too, in a quiet way."

Isaac returned to Trinity. He felt very good indeed!

CHAPTER ELEVEN:

Gravity at Last

Trinity College and Isaac Newton seemed to have been made for each other. Trinity supplied him with everything he needed. An elderly maid named Deborah cleaned his room. A Sizar carried food to him when he worked late. An assistant, Humphrey Newton by name (they were not related), helped with experiments.

In return Isaac brought fame and honor to the school. But Newton's greatest triumph was still to come. The story began in London, sixty miles away. While Isaac worked alone at Trinity, groups of men in London met together each week to talk about exciting rumors that made the rounds in scientific circles.

One afternoon in January 1684, three men entered a coffee house near the Royal Exchange building in London. They had come from a meeting of the Royal Society.

Sir Christopher Wren, the oldest of the three, was known by sight by most of the people in London. He chose a private table in the corner. He motioned for the two men with him to take chairs. He asked, "What shall we talk about today?"

One of the men with Wren was Robert Hooke. He had not changed much in the last twenty years. He still had a rough voice, ungroomed hair, thin face, and irritable manner. In a hoarse whisper he said, "*Gravity.*"

The third man seated with them was Edmund Halley, a young astronomer. He had made his mark while an astronomy student in college. Astronomy textbooks and star charts were a blank as far as southern stars were concerned. Professional astronomers had not observed them properly. Before finishing college Halley impulsively packed a telescope and took a ship to the desolate island of St. Helena. There he plotted the position of stars not visible from England. When he returned, the Royal Society elected him a member.

Halley said, "I agree with our friend Hooke. Gravity is the most important unsolved problem in science today."

Wren nodded agreement. "Every astronomer and mathematician has played with the idea. I am convinced that gravity grows weaker by the square of the distance—a planet twice as far from the sun would be pulled by a force that is only one-fourth as great."

Hooke said, "Yes, I believe that."

Halley smiled ruefully. "Easy to say, but difficult to prove. Kepler showed that a planet travels around the sun in an ellipse. A real law of gravity would show why the planets follow an ellipse and not a circle."

"The inverse square law is true!" Hooke said. "Only a fool would doubt it."

"But only a genius could prove it," Wren pointed out.

Halley agreed. "It is a knotty problem. I have had a terrible time with it. Long ago I threw up my hands in defeat. Someone else will have to prove it."

Wren looked to Hooke, "Do you admit defeat?"

Hooke smiled a twisted smile. "Quite the contrary. I have a proof. I can show that gravity causes the planets to travel in elliptical orbits."

"Then show your proof to us!" Halley demanded.

Hooke said, "I wish to keep my discovery to myself for the time being."

"But why?" Halley asked. "It is too important to hold back. Many secrets of nature are
waiting to be understood."

Hooke said, "When others try and fail, they
will understand the value of my discovery when
I make it public."

Wren looked at Hooke closely. Was he telling
the truth? Wren couldn't be certain. Hooke had
a habit of jumping to conclusions without the
facts to back up his guesses. Wren didn't openly
express his doubts. He said, "Let me encourage
you to present a solution immediately. I will
give Mr. Hooke, or you Mr. Halley, two months in
which to bring me a solution. When you do, I
will present you with an expensive book worth at
least forty shillings. And I'll see to it that your
solution is brought before the Royal Society. The
fame for its discovery will be yours alone."

Hooke said, "You will have your proof."

Halley returned to his home in Islington. Even
he took up the problem again. But he reached a
dead end.

Two months passed. Halley waited, anxious
for Hooke to come forward with the proof.

Wren shook his head at their next meeting. "He
was not good to his word. Hooke has no solution."

Halley made a sudden decision. "I am going
to Cambridge to see Isaac Newton."

"Newton? Why Newton?" Wren asked.

"Because he has an experimental mind trained
both in astronomy and mathematics."

Wren said doubtfully, "Everybody agrees he is
a great natural philosopher."

Halley shook his head. "Isaac Newton is not a
great scientist. You, my dear Wren, are a great
scientist. Our friend Hooke is a great scientist.
But Newton, well, he is more than great. He is the
finest mind ever produced. I'm certain of that."

Halley traveled to Cambridge. He found Isaac working in his study.

Halley introduced himself. "Let me come at once to the point of my visit. What would be the curve described by the planets on the supposition that gravity diminishes as the square of the distance?"

Newton immediately answered, "An ellipse."

Halley was struck with joy and amazement. He asked, "How do you know it?"

"Why, I have calculated it," Isaac explained.

"I must see the calculations," Halley said. He could hardly believe his good fortune. "How long have you had the solution?"

Isaac said, "I first began looking into gravity at Woolsthorpe during the Black Death. I spent a year or so there working upon many things, including the law of gravitation. But the answer didn't come out right. Pretty nearly—but not close enough to suit me."

"Tell me about it," Halley insisted.

"You see," Isaac said, "I came to believe that the force of gravity acted on the moon in the same way as it did on a falling apple. There was room to doubt, so I chose to not tell about my results. Then, about five years ago, a better set of figures came to light. I set out to do the calculations again. This time I met with success."

"Where are the calculations!" Halley cried.

"It has been so long ago," Isaac said. He began going through his desk. "I think I threw the paper in this drawer." He pulled out a fist full of wrinkled papers. He looked through them and shook his head.

Isaac arose and stood in the middle of the room, trying to remember. "Perhaps Deborah accidentally swept it away. Well, the paper is lost."

Halley could hardly contain himself. He begged Isaac to search for the paper until he found it.

Isaac said, "The paper itself is not important. I can do the calculations again."

Halley said, "I will not leave here unless you promise to find the original paper or do the work again."

Isaac smiled at the earnest young man. Halley had an easy smile and infectious nature that could not be put down. "Very well," Isaac said. "I will do the work again and send it to you in London."

Three months later Isaac finished the new proof. He sent the work to London by a young mathematician named Paget who agreed to act as messenger. The mail system couldn't be trusted.

Isaac explained the delay. "I was held up for some time by a careless mistake in one of the diagrams."

At first Halley hardly knew what to make of the

packet of notes. Isaac had hastily scribbled on odds and ends of paper, both the front and back.

Halley waded through the finely written proof. He sat back in wonder. He took the paper to Wren. "The proof is complete. Isaac Newton has proven what other men have only guessed. The sun, the moon, the planets—even apples and grains of sand—all attract each other according to a simple equation."

Christopher Wren said, "I wonder how many other great ideas are hidden away in his mind."

Halley said, "You are right. Isaac Newton does not recognize his own genius. Complex problems are simple to him. He works them out to his own satisfaction, then he puts them aside without telling anyone."

Wren said, "What a waste!"

Halley said, "Newton's discoveries must be brought out to see the light of day."

Halley traveled to Cambridge again. He explained to Newton, "You must put all of your discoveries in the form of a book."

Isaac Newton didn't think much of that idea. "A man who serves science must be willing to engage in lawsuits and petty quibbling. I share my discoveries with the students at Trinity."

Halley, however, would not take no for an answer. He knew he couldn't tempt Isaac with fame or glory. So he appealed to their friendship. "Your discoveries are important to me and other astronomers who are trying to figure out the paths of planets and comets."

Isaac Newton shook his head. "The time needed to see a book through to the printer would keep me from my study of Scripture."

Halley suddenly pounced upon an idea. "Then let me attend to all of the bothersome details. You write the manuscript. I will see that the illustrations are made. I will take the manuscript to the printer and correct the galley proofs. I will take care of everything!"

Halley's excitement was infectious. Issac could resist no longer. Why, Halley talked as if it would be a great adventure! Isaac felt himself stir with excitement.

"You will have your book," Isaac said.

Halley returned to London to spread the good news. "Mr. Newton has promised to write a full account of his discoveries!"

During the first days of 1685, Isaac cleared his desk and prepared for the awesome job ahead. He would be plunging into an area of discovery where no man had gone before.

During the eighteen months that followed Halley's visit, Isaac worked day and night on the book. He didn't mind the sacrifice. A living, growing thing took shape before his eyes. Never mind that he ate irregularly. Never mind if he kept at it eighteen hours a day. The book would be worth all the effort.

He called the book *Principia Mathematica Philosophiae Naturalis.* This is Latin of course. Scientists all over the world knew Latin. Newton decided to use that language. People in other countries could read his book at once without waiting for it to be translated into French, German or other languages. The title meant "Mathematical Principles of Natural Philosophy." He and Halley called it simply *Principia.*

Isaac looked for a grand pattern to the universe. He spent long periods lost in thought. Then suddenly he dashed off several pages without pausing. As he wrote, new ideas sprang up and poured out on the paper.

Meals remained uneaten. Sleep was forgotten. He seldom left his room.

Deborah clucked her tongue. "I bring him food. But he leaves it on the table by the door. He doesn't eat." She shook her head.

Humphrey silenced the woman. Edmund Halley was coming up the stairs. Humphrey said, "Mr. Halley, it is a pleasure to see you."

"How is the book coming?" Halley asked.

"He has finished the first part, and I am making a clean copy right now, but I need help with the illustrations."

"How is Mr. Newton?" Halley asked.

Humphrey pulled Halley to one side. "He rarely goes to bed until two or three of the clock, sometimes not until five or six. He is completely absorbed with the book."

Halley entered the chambers. He found Isaac sitting on his bed, a blanket thrown over his shoulders. He had a thin face, eyes with a tired

look in them. He was completely still, lost in thought.

Halley waited for Isaac to notice him.

"Oh, Halley, my friend!" Isaac said. His eyes lighted up in pleasure. "Come in and have a seat. There is food on the table. You can have it."

Halley asked, "What were you thinking upon?"

Isaac said, "I fear my book will not be understood."

"And why would that be?" Halley asked.

"Gravity explains the motions of the planets, but it cannot explain who set the planets in motion. God governs all things, and knows all that is or can be done. God is the final cause, this we know. He certainly belongs in natural philosophy."

Halley said, "Maybe you can add a section at the end of the book and sum up both your scientific and religious beliefs."

Newton nodded in an absent-minded way. "The book is already too long."

Isaac had divided the *Principia* into three books. In the first book he laid down three laws of motion.

LAW ONE: *A body at rest will remain at rest unless acted upon by an outside force. A body in motion will continue with the same speed and direction unless acted upon by an outside force.*

LAW TWO: *The change in motion of a body depends upon the mass of the body and the force acting upon it.*

The second law defines force in terms of mass and change in speed. Mass and weight are not quite the same thing because the weight of a body can change when it moves from the earth to, say, the moon. The mass of a body is always the same even when it is weightless out in space.

Newton was the first scientist to show that there
was a difference between the mass of a body and
its weight.

LAW THREE: *For every action there is an
equal and opposite reaction.*

This is an important principle. The law of reaction explains why a rocket works. A rocket flies
away when lighted. The gas spewing out from
the end shoots the rocket forward. This is the
only way to cross the vacuum of space.

In addition to the three laws of motion Newton stated the Law of Universal Gravitation
which can best be given in the form of an equation: $F = \dfrac{Mm}{d^2}$ According to this every body in
the universe attracts every other body by a force
that depends upon the masses of the bodies and
the distance that separates them.

The second book of the *Principia* showed how
to use the three laws of motion and the law of
gravity to work out the masses of the sun and the
planets and to find their distances.

Halley could hardly wait for Isaac to finish
the third book. In it he would show how to calculate the paths of comets. He also intended to
explain tides.

Isaac finished the first two books of *Principia*,
and Halley took them to the printers. Then, just
as Isaac finished the third book, Halley sent a
letter. The letter contained disturbing news.

Robert Hooke again! Halley said, "Mr. Hooke
pretends that it was he who invented the law of
gravity. Mr. Hooke seems to expect that you
should make some mention of him in the preface
of *Principia*."

Isaac looked into the charges that Hooke was
making. "He not only claims credit for the inverse square law, but he actually claims that I

stole it from him! The manuscript is in your hands. There is not one sentence of the *Principia* which he can pretend to be his. I do not see any proper reason for mentioning him there."

Isaac decided, "I will put aside the third book. It is better to do that than engage in useless arguments."

Halley, of course, was aghast. He quickly traveled to Trinity to calm Newton. Halley said, "Hooke sat idly by while you did the work. But you must remember that he is bitter and angry. The first two books of the *Principia* have caused him to lose power and status."

He pointed out that it would not hurt Isaac to mention Hooke. "The entire scientific world knows that you, and you alone, deserve credit. Hooke's ideas were vague and completely disorganized."

Isaac slowly calmed down. In the end he agreed to Halley's suggestion. He added a line to the preface of the *Principia* in which he agreed that Sir Christopher Wren, Dr. Hooke, and Dr. Halley had already put forth the inverse square law.

The *Principia* was officially presented to the Royal Society on April 28, 1686. Due to poor management the Society had no funds. They could not pay the cost of having the *Principia* printed.

Halley had promised Isaac that he would see that the book was published. Halley offered to pay the cost of having it printed. It was a difficult decision for him. He lived with his wife and child in near poverty.

To Halley's delight, the book sold quickly. It sold so well, in fact, he not only got his money back, but he made a profit as well.

The *Principia* was a masterpiece, produced by

a mastermind. A German scientist called Newton the foremost mathematician of his time. In
France a scientist said, "The work of Mr. Newton
is the most perfect treatise that can be imagined."

To this day the *Principia* is generally looked
upon as the greatest scientific work ever written.

Halley read Isaac's section on comets. "Universal? You expect your law of gravity to apply
to comets as well as planets?"

"Certainly," Newton answered his young friend.
"Nature is pleased with simplicity. The three
laws of motion and the Universal Law of Gravitation apply to all things everywhere; to an apple
falling from a tree, to a cannon ball rolling down
an incline, to the moon moving around the earth
—even to those comets that interest you."

Halley said, "The motions of the planets are
easy to predict. But comets can whip into view
at any time from any direction. Then they dis-
appear, never to be seen again."

"Ah," Isaac said. "How do you know they are
never seen again? All comets look alike. It is my
belief that they travel in long elliptical orbits.
A single trip around the sun takes many years. It
may be a lifetime or even longer."

Halley said, "I saw a bright comet in the year
1682. When it returns, if it does, I will not be
alive to see it."

"That is true," Isaac agreed. "But if comets are
regular visitors as I believe they are, then the
comet of 1682 must have visited us more than
once in the past."

Halley began to look back through old books
and ancient records. He made a list of all the
bright comets. A bright comet had been seen in
1531, 1607, and 1682. Seventy-six years apart!
Halley boldly suggested that it was not three
separate comets, but the same comet seen time

and again.

He predicted the return of "his" comet in 1758. He knew that he would be dead by then, but he expressed the hope that if it did indeed appear as he predicted, then people would acknowledge that this was first discovered by an Englishman using Newton's Law of Universal Gravitation.

(He was right, of course. For the first time in history a comet was expected to appear during 1758. On Christmas night, sixteen years after the death of Halley, an astronomer spotted the faithful visitor. Named Halley's Comet it is expected again in 1986.)

The Law of Universal Gravitation explained the behavior of planets and comets, but Newton believed the hand of God supervised the solar system. He said, "This most beautiful system of sun, planets, and comets could only proceed from the counsel and dominion of an intelligent and powerful being."

The *Principia* was not easy reading. Isaac intentionally made it hard so that only those with a real interest and skill could read it. "Those who only smatter in mathematics will not be able to bait me with silly questions," he explained. However, Isaac did write a short summary which he included in the third part of *Principia*.

The fame of Isaac and his book spread throughout the world. One student pointed him out and said, "There goes the man who wrote a book that neither he nor anyone else understands."

The English poet Alexandria Pope wrote a famous couplet:

Nature and Nature's laws lay hid in nights:
God said, Let Newton be! and all was light.

Isaac Newton, humble as ever, said, "If I have seen further than other men, it is by standing on the shoulders of giants."

CHAPTER TWELVE:

MENE, MENE, TEKEL, UPHARSIN

Charles II died in 1685 after serving England as Monarch for twenty-five years. He was kind and tolerant and full of good humor, although his character was not without blemish. During his rule the hard feelings of the Civil War faded away. England changed into a country whose citizens worked together.

All of this came tumbling down upon his death. James II, his brother, took his place as King. James II believed a king had absolute power. He believed he could do whatever he wished without following any laws.

In particular, he believed the King could decide the religion of the people of England. James II was a Roman Catholic. He openly declared that he would change England back to that religion.

James II could have worshiped in his own way and left everyone else alone. Even the Roman Catholics feared his action. They had lived with their Protestant neighbors in peace. Suppose James II failed. They would be in trouble because the Protestants outnumbered them.

But James II refused to listen to reason. He began to dismiss Protestants from high office and put Catholics who supported him in their place.

Many of those he put in office had no real ability in the positions they filled.

Cambridge University watched the changes with mounting alarm. If James II planned upon making the country Catholic, then he would soon change the colleges where clergymen were trained.

And he did. James II ordered the University to grant Father Alban Francis a Master of Arts degree. Father Francis, a Catholic, had not studied at Cambridge. He did not have the qualifications.

But if he were granted the degree, then he would be able to vote in the College Senate.

The King's strategy became clear. He planned to "pack" the University Senate with Catholic Fellows. They would then vote to change the University charter to make the school Catholic.

The University officials turned down the King's command. They refused to grant the degree.

King James II plotted a cruel revenge. He charged the University with contempt. He summoned the Vice-Chancellor and eight representatives before the High Court. Judge Jeffreys ruled over the High Court.

Judge Jeffreys could only be described as one of the most unpleasant figures of all time. Only a few months earlier he had calmly ordered more than three hundred men to be hanged until dead. Everyone feared him; no one liked him. He was a cruel, sarcastic bully.

The Vice-Chancellor of Cambridge, Dr. John Pechell, and eight other men were chosen to go to London. They would give Judge Jeffreys the reason for not granting a degree to Father Francis.

Isaac Newton was one of the eight.

Before leaving for London the men came to-

gether to decide what to do. A cloud of dread
hung over the meeting. Judge Jeffreys could be
depended upon to be harsh and wrathful. The
delegates wanted to find a way to compromise.
They feared for their very lives.

While the others talked about how to word
the compromise, Isaac stood and began walking
around the room. After taking several turns, Isaac
strode to the table.

"This is giving up the question," he said.

"How do you mean?" Vice-Chancellor Pechell
asked. He was a timid man.

"The University must stand firm. Our cause is
right. The law is on our side." Isaac was very
much against any kind of interference with the
religion of others.

"What do you suggest that we do?" one member of the committee asked.

Isaac said, "We should prepare a paper which
sets forth our position."

Vice-Chancellor Pechell reluctantly agreed.
The others went along, too. But Judge Jeffreys and the High Court terrified them.

Judge Jeffreys let them stew for ten days before he called them before him. He looked over
the group and swooped down on the weakest
man—Vice-Chancellor Pechell.

He treated Pechell with contempt. He asked
questions and demanded answers before Pechell
could reply. He reduced the man to stuttering.
Then he made fun of him.

"You claim to be the Vice-Chancellor of Cambridge University. Then repeat to me your oath
of office!" Jeffreys demanded.

By this time Pechell was completely paralyzed
with fear.

Another member stood, "I will repeat the oath
for him."

"Sit down!" Jeffreys thundered. "Clear the courtroom. I will speak with Vice-Chancellor Pechell alone."

The other committee members filed from the courtroom. They were worried about Pechell. He didn't have the strength to reply to the abuse Judge Jeffreys heaped upon him.

As the men met outside the courtroom, Isaac went from man to man and spoke with them. He gave them the backbone to resist the Royal command.

Finally they were allowed to reenter the High Court. Vice-Chancellor Pechell had been too nervous and frightened to speak. Instead, he had turned in the written paper explaining the University's legal stand.

Judge Jeffreys read the paper. He tossed it back like it was a worthless scrap of paper. He tried to show his contempt. But he knew the University had a strong legal case, and they had it in writing. He would not be able to force them to bend to the King's will.

Judge Jeffreys turned scarlet. He gave the entire committee a harsh tongue-lashing. He threatened all sorts of terrible penalties. But in the end he took the only legal action in his power. He removed Vice-Chancellor Pechell from office.

Judge Jeffreys' plan was to replace Pechell with someone more willing to go along with the King's program.

He figured wrong. The new Vice-Chancellor, John Balderston, was a strong man. He stood up for the University. Father Alban Francis never received his Master's degree.

The leaders of Cambridge University held their breaths in dread. How would James II strike back?

But James II had made too many enemies. The people didn't like his high handed ways. Tampering with the University had been the last straw.

The country's leaders invited Prince William of Orange and his wife Mary Stuart to come to England and rule as King and Queen.

James II called for help to put down the rebels. No one stood with him. He fled the country to save his life. The rest of his life was spent in France in exile.

Judge Jeffreys tried to escape, too. He dressed up as a common sailor. But he was caught in a tavern. While in power he acted like a bully, now he showed himself to be a coward. He was thrown in the Tower and died there while awaiting trial. This ended a short, but terrible, time in

England's history.

Parliament was called into session again. One representative would go to Parliament from the University. Who should it be?

Isaac Newton was not a politician, and he seemed an unlikely choice. But everyone was impressed by his calm, strong leadership during the trial. In 1689 Isaac Newton was seated in the House of Commons.

He said little during the public sessions. In fact, he arose only once to speak. The House grew silent to listen to what the great man had to say. He asked that a window be closed because there was a draft.

Behind the scenes, however, he worked as a dedicated friend of civil and religious freedom.

One of Isaac's best friends in Parliament was Charles Montague, a former student at Trinity. Charles Montague was an ambitious young man who rose quickly in politics and became a leader of the Whig Party.

Isaac Newton confided in his friend. "The time has come for me to seek a change. Parliament will dissolve soon, once the country settles down. When that happens, I would like to have a government position. Would you look for a suitable post?"

Charles Montague agreed to help, but he warned Isaac, "You must understand that government matters move slowly. Don't be disappointed if I fail right away. It takes time."

Charles Montague looked at his friend closely. "Why do you seek an administrative job?"

Isaac said, "I am exhausted after writing the *Principia*. Science does not hold the interest that it once did. So many of my friends have died. Isaac Barrow, John Collins, Henry Oldenburg—they are all gone. I need a change."

About this time sad news arrived from Benjamin Smith, Isaac's half brother. He lived at Stamford, a town about fifteen miles from Woolsthorpe. The letter from Benjamin said, "Our mother is gravely ill."

Isaac rushed to Stamford. Benjamin told what had happened. "I came down with a high fever about three months ago. Hannah attended to me during the illness. I got well, but she came down with the same disease. We have been unable to help her."

"I will attend to her," Isaac said. He stayed by her bedside both day and night. He placed soothing ointments on the blisters that broke out over her body. He changed the dressings and tried as best he could to ease her suffering.

Weeks passed. Isaac watched helpless as she grew weaker. On June 4, 1689, Hannah Newton Smith died. It was Isaac's sad duty to go with the body back to the family church at Colsterworth for burial.

Early in 1690, Parliament dissolved. The representatives went back home. For five years Isaac had been working eighteen hours a day. Suddenly he found himself with nothing to do. *What lies ahead of me?* he thought. *What shall*

I do?

Isaac rode back to Trinity. He walked the lonely stairway to his room. He waited for a letter from Charles Montague about a government position in London. But Charles Montague had to write Isaac and tell of his failure. "The Whig Party is out of power at the moment. I have been unable to locate a post for you. But England owes you a post of honor for your great work."

Isaac entered the darkest days of his life. His health failed. For several months he huddled on the floor in front of the fire and tried to rest. But regular sleep did not come. He felt cold and alone. Cold chills shook his body one moment to be replaced by sudden fevers that drenched him in sweat the next moment.

His mind, too, suffered strange nightmares in which he thought his friends had forsaken him.

Isaac could not think clearly. Everything became confused. He wrote letters in which he accused his friends of doing all sorts of terrible deeds against him.

His friends—Locke, Pepys, Halley and Montague—read the letters and put them aside. They did not become angry. They knew he was under a great emotional strain since the death of his mother.

Isaac Newton had reason to be mentally exhausted. The writing of the *Principia* would have broken a normal man. Following that was the dangerous affair with Judge Jeffreys. For a person who disliked disputes the last five years had been filled with one conflict after another.

Locke tried to steer Isaac back to an interest in life. He wrote letters and asked questions about Bible history.

Isaac began spending more time reading and studying the Bible. He spent many hours tracing

down old manuscripts about the Bible. Through
weeks of strain and sleepless nights, his study of
the Bible and his faith in Christ as his Saviour
carried Isaac through the shadow of fear and the
time of doubt. The dark days passed. Newton
recovered. His mind was as sharp as ever, his
faith in the Lord strong and sure.

His first order of business was to write his
long-suffering friends and apologize to them. In
a letter to Locke he said, "I am very much
ashamed for the rudeness I showed to my friends.
I owe you an apology. When I wrote to you, I
had not slept an hour a night for a fortnight
(two weeks) together, and for five nights together
not a wink."

After he mailed the letters of apology, he felt
much better. Everyone could sometimes be foolish. The darkness of the world is but a shadow,
but there is light that causes the shadow. Isaac
Newton decided to turn to the light.

He relaxed for the first time in many years. He
turned to his boyhood hobbies of making models.

Edmund Halley called upon Isaac. He wanted
to inquire about Isaac's health and ask him to
put out a new edition of the *Principia*.

"Come in, Halley!" Isaac said.

Halley saw that Isaac was thin and pale, but
his eyes were bright with interest. Halley
breathed easier. He had heard stories about
Isaac's illness. But his friend seemed to be his
old self.

"What are you working upon?" Halley asked.

Isaac was fitting a circle of iron to a square
board. "A sundial," Isaac explained. "Students
who know how to use it can tell both the time of
day using the sun and the time of night by
using the moon."

"And what is this," Halley asked. He pointed

to a sheet of paper tacked to the wall. On it
was a charcoal sketch of an arch bridge. "It
looks like a footbridge. You haven't taken up
architecture have you? I will have to warn our
friend Wren that you intend to put him out of
business."

"No," Isaac said. "But it is an interesting di-
version. This is a bridge which fits together without nails."

Halley came to the purpose of his visit. "You
should be thinking about changes to be made in
the next edition of the *Principia*. The booksellers
say they have sold all of the new copies, and
used copies are difficult to find."

Isaac shook his head. "I am not ready at this
time to work on a new edition."

Newton did not become ready to write the
next edition for almost twenty years. He added
to it a section which read in part, "The true God
is a living, intelligent, and powerful being. His
duration reaches from eternity to eternity; his
presence from infinity to infinity. He governs all
things."

Isaac said good-bye to Halley and settled down
to a long period of relaxed study in which he
put all of his religious ideas together. Religious
matters had been on his mind for most of his
life. After all, he had come to Cambridge with
the expectation of becoming a minister and taking a rural parish.

One of the books he worked upon now was
Chronology of Ancient Kingdoms. In this book
he used his knowledge of astronomy and clues
from the Bible to find the dates of important
events such as the Flood and when Moses led
the Children of Israel from slavery in Egypt. He
used his skill with mathematics to figure out the
size of a cubit. The cubit is a measurement of

length. It was used to give the size of the Hebrew
Temple and Noah's Ark.

Isaac also worked upon another book called
Observations Upon the Prophecies of Daniel. He
recalled the book that first interested him in
Daniel. His stepfather had given it to him long
ago.

As he had learned in his Bible class at King's
school, Daniel was a Hebrew prince who was
captured and taken to Babylon. There he was
trained as a servant of King Nebuchadnezzar.

Daniel rose in power because God gave him
the ability to tell the meaning of dreams. During a feast of Belshazzar (who became king after
Nebuchadnezzar) a mysterious hand appeared
and wrote four words on the palace wall. The
words were: MENE, MENE, TEKEL, UPHAR-
SIN.

Isaac read again the thrilling story of how Daniel correctly told the meaning of the strange
writing. Daniel said the handwriting on the wall
meant that God had weighed Belshazzar in the
balances and found him wanting. Before the
night ended Darius, the King of the Medes, attacked the palace. Belshazzar died in the fighting.

Besides telling an exciting story, the Book of
Daniel contains many difficult passages of Scripture which seem to point to events which were
to take place in the future.

But Isaac Newton did not try to use the Prophecies to predict the future. He believed this a
mistake. He explained in his book, "The folly
of interpreters has been to foretell times and
things. The design of God was much otherwise.
God gave the prophecies of the Old Testament
that after they were fulfilled they might become
intelligible. The prophecies afford convincing ar-

gument that the world is governed by Providence."

The two books together, *Ancient Kingdoms* and *Observations Upon the Prophecies* make a connected history of the world from creation until the end of time.

A young Bible scholar named Richard Bently came to Isaac Newton for help with a series of lectures that he was giving in London.

He explained, "As you know Robert Boyle provided money for a series of lectures to provide proofs of the existence of God."

Isaac nodded, "He often said that scientists should speak up about their beliefs. And I agree. Atheism is so senseless. When I look at the solar system, I see the earth at the right distance from the sun to receive the proper amounts of heat and light. This did not happen by chance. The motions of the planets require a Divine arm to impress them."

Newton had entirely recovered from his dark days. He wanted to get back into action. Charles Montague had been elected President of the Royal Society. Not only that, but his party, the Whigs, had come back into power. Maybe this time Charles Montague would be able to help.

On March 19, 1696, Montague wrote to Isaac. A note of triumph was in the letter:

Sir,
  I am very glad that at last I can give you good proof of my friendship. The King has promised me to make Mr. Newton Warden of the Mint. The Office is most proper for you. 'Tis the chief officer in the Mint. . . . I believe you may have lodging near me. I am, Sir, your most obedient servant,

                                    Chas. Montague.

Newton looked out of his second floor window at the students rushing to classes. It would be strange to awaken to the sound of traffic upon London's streets instead of the sound of school. For twenty-seven years Trinity had been his home. Now it was time to move along to other things.

"But I shall not retire!" he resolved. "I will not be put on pension. There are still things to do."

CHAPTER THIRTEEN:

"Paw of the Lion"

As soon as Newton was appointed Warden of the Mint he moved to London. He was taking a perfectly ordinary government post, but he was taking it at a most extraordinary time. The coinage of the country was in a very bad state. England's business life was based upon gold and silver coins. Paper money was seldom used.

Most of the coins were crudely made and in miserable shape. Some had been handed from person to person for a hundred years or more. Day to day wear had made them lose value, but a more sinister cause was dishonest people. They saw a fast way to make money by clipping off the edges of the coins. The coins weighed nowhere near their true weight.

Newton found a place to live near Montague's home. After getting settled he stopped at a bookstore to look for new books which he had been unable to find in Cambridge. Near the front of the store two men were in a heated argument.

"Here! What is the problem?" Isaac asked.

"Well, look at this," the customer said. "The bookseller demands payment for my order with coins of full weight, but these coins are official coins put out by the government."

Isaac weighed one of the coins in his hand. "But this coin has only half its regular weight. Someone is being cheated."

"We are all being cheated," the store owner said. "All of the coins are dishonest. It is even worse on Saturday night when I pay my employees for their week's work. They don't like these underweight coins, and I can understand how they feel. Who would want to be paid with shilling pieces that are only worth six pence?"

The two men haggled over the price of the book. The buyer insisted upon going by face value. The seller just as definitely insisted upon taking the silver coins by their weight. A simple purchase turned into a serious quarrel.

Charles Montague, the Chancellor of the Exchequer, agreed with Newton that the monetary system was in a sad shape. "It is a mess," he admitted. "The old coins are very thin and the edges are not marked with milling. Dishonest people take advantage of the crudely minted coins and chip off the edges. We put out new coins. But instead of using them, the people store them away or melt them down and sell the silver to jewelers. The bad money keeps the good money off the market."

Newton said, "Then the old coins must be recalled."

Charles Montague said, "We can't recall all of the old coins at once. If we did there wouldn't be enough money to use in the market places."

Newton considered the problem. "Then the only thing to do is to remove the poor coins and at the same time put out new ones."

"Yes," Charles Montague said, "the recoinage act gives me the power to do just that. During the next few months we will make thousands of new coins. Then, during the summer, we will flood London with new coins. At the same time we will take in the poor ones. We will pay face value for them."

The government will lose money," Isaac said.

"Yes, but it can't be helped," Montague said. "I'm certain we can think up a new tax to make up the difference! If the recoinage plan is successful we will set a date after which chipped or badly worn coins will no longer be accepted."

"How do I fit into this?" Isaac Newton asked.

"You are an expert with metals, and you are skilled in mathematics. Most important of all, the people will trust the great Isaac Newton. They know you are honest. Trust is important. Every coin in England will be remade. Hundreds of tons of silver will pass through your hands in the next four months. Every ounce of it must be accounted for."

Isaac walked to the mint where he inspected ten furnaces newly built in the gardens behind the Treasury. The furnaces melted worn coins and cast the silver into shiny ingots. Workmen hauled the ingots into the mint. There horse powered presses stamped the metal into coins.

Newton watched over the melting of old coins and the stamping of new ones. This took a lot of business ability and hard work. He kept a double set of books for all the money that passed through his hands. Before he took over, mint officials pointed with pride to weeks in which they changed fifteen thousand pounds of silver into coins. Newton did four times as well.

But despite his best efforts, shortages of money came up during the summer months. Isaac talked to groups of citizens.

"I promise," Isaac told them, "that the shortage will not last long."

"We trust your judgment," they said. "We believe you will soon solve the problem."

Isaac asked for trusted friends to come to the aid of their country. He called upon Edmund Halley. "To keep my word, I have opened branch mints outside of London. I must ask for you to take charge of one of them."

"I will serve you well," Halley agreed.

"The work must be done quickly and correctly," Isaac said. "We cannot favor any one person or any one place with new coins. The coins must be put out fairly."

Weeks later Isaac reported to Charles Montague. "Production has doubled. A hundred thousand pounds of silver a week are being changed into coins."

Charles Montague said, "This tremendous undertaking will make changes in the English monetary system that will last for more than a hundred years."

"It has not been easy for my men," Isaac said. "Old employees do not like the changes we have had to make. Dishonest business men who want special treatment have tried to bribe them with so called 'gifts.' One branch officer was challenged to a duel."

Charles Montague said, "But the recoinage is going successfully."

"Yes, except for a serious rash of counterfeit coins which have suddenly appeared on the market. It seems to be the work of a master criminal."

Charles Montague viewed the matter with alarm. "He must be stopped! You must track down the criminal who is putting out the debased money."

Newton had already become a detective. He said, "I have organized a network of agents who are going out to get facts."

"But your men will be recognized," Charles Montague objected.

"No," Isaac said. "I have given them disguises. They will go to the poorer sections of town and talk to barbers, pawn brokers, and tavern owners."

The network of agents that Isaac organized brought in suspects for interviews. Isaac questioned the criminals, too. His sharp eyes and quick mind pounced upon those who tried to lie. He read through hundreds of reports in search for clues.

Slowly he closed in on the evil character behind the phony money.

Isaac said, "The counterfeiter is William Chaloner."

"Why, I know him," Charles Montague said. "He goes about London as a wealthy gentleman."

"It is a pose," Isaac said. "William Chaloner has powerful friends in high places in government. He has fooled them into thinking he is honest. But London's underworld knows Chaloner as the prince of thieves."

"But he is rich," Montague said.

Isaac explained, "I have learned how he became rich. Many years ago, when he was poor and unknown, he turned in two printers for printing illegal documents. But I have found out that Chaloner himself paid the men to print the illegal papers. Then he went to the government and turned them in. Not only did government officials praise him, they gave him a huge reward as well. He used the money to buy expensive clothes and a fancy home at Knightsbridge."

Charles Montague struck his fist against the palm of his hand. "He must be brought to justice!"

At first Isaac failed to bring Chaloner to court. Chaloner plotted to hide his criminal activities and to put friends into places of trust inside the mint itself.

Isaac Newton started at the bottom with petty thieves. They confessed their crimes and gave the names of others who worked for Chaloner. Slowly Newton worked higher and higher to more important men.

Then came the big break. Thomas Holloway, Chaloner's righthand man and fellow criminal, broke down under questioning and admitted to their deeds.

Chaloner thought his political friends would protect him. During his trial he laughed and smiled.

Isaac Newton pushed for conviction. He gave his reasons. "I believe it is better to let him suffer than to let him go on to counterfeit the coins and teach others to do so as well. These people seldom leave off."

The trial ended. "Guilty" echoed in the courtroom. The jury had found Chaloner guilty of many crimes, including high treason.

With the successful completion of the recoinage plan, Isaac Newton was promoted to Master of the Mint. Now he needed someone to help run his busy household, and he sent for his niece, Catherine Barton. She was the granddaughter of Newton's mother. He adored her, and she loved him.

Although Catherine was only nineteen years old, she had charm and beauty and wit that made her a favorite with everyone she met. Soon the Jermyn Street home of Isaac Newton became a favorite meeting place for the best in London's society. Renowned scientists from all over the world came to talk with Isaac Newton and meet the young lady.

Many people had the mistaken belief that Newton's scholarship days were over. They believed his mind had grown weak.

The famous Swiss mathematician Jean Bernoulli proposed a difficult problem which even the best mathematicians would have trouble solving. He gave six months for a full solution. The time limit had to be extended by a year because no one solved the problem completely.

Isaac had been busy at the mint and did not hear of the problem until one afternoon when he came in from work.

Catherine Barton said, "Charles Montague sent a note from the Royal Society. It's a puzzle European mathematicians have been unable to solve."

"Well, let an Englishman look at it," Isaac said. He checked the time. It was four o'clock. The problem asked for the shape of a curve that would let a ball roll along the curve between two points in the shortest amount of time.

Isaac Newton solved the problem before going to bed! He turned in the solution, but he did not sign his name to it.

Jean Bernoulli, however, was not fooled. He said, "I see the paw of the lion!"

With the successful completion of the recoinage program, Isaac had time to take on other duties. For example, he served in Parliament again for a short time in 1701.

Soon after his term in Parliament ended, the English scientists offered him the post of President of the Royal Society. Although Isaac retained his position at the Mint, he agreed to serve as President as well.

When he took the office, Isaac felt it was his duty to return to a more active role in scientific studies. He gathered his notes and experiments about light and put them together in a book called *Opticks*.

Edmund Halley was surprised when he received a copy. "This is nothing like the *Principia!*

It is written in an easy to read style, and in English, too!"

Isaac Newton explained, "Some people complained that the *Principia* left nothing for others to do. Well, there is still plenty to do in the study of light. At the back of the book I have listed the questions that I have not yet been able to answer."

Opticks was rich with ideas. In a short section of twelve pages he brought out two dozen important ideas.

But his greatest honor came in 1705 when Queen Anne informed him that he would be knighted. It would be the first knighthood for scientific discovery rather than deeds on the battlefield. Isaac Newton won knighthood because he carried a pen and not a sword.

To show that the honor was for his advances in learning, Queen Anne and her entire court traveled to Trinity. There in the assembly hall before a fireplace she touched a sword to Isaac Newton's shoulder.

Queen Anne said, "It is a great happiness to have lived at the same time, and to have known, so great a man."

Sir Isaac Newton! The country boy from Woolsthorpe had come a long way.

Sir Isaac Newton ended his days surrounded by friends and loved ones and honored by his country. He died Monday, March 20, 1727, between one and two o'clock in the morning. Although Isaac had been a frail person at birth, he grew up in good health. He died at the age of eighty-five, still with a full head of hair, sharp eyesight, and all his teeth save one.

England tried to show the great honor in which he was held. The people mourned his death. His body rested in the Jerusalem Chamber of Westminister Abby.

The burial plot had been reserved for a king. Never before or since has a country honored a scholar in such a way. England treated Isaac the way other countries treated kings.

The memorial stone above the grave reads:

Mortals!
Rejoice at so great an ornament
to the human race!

But what did Newton have to say about himself? Shortly before his death he said, "I do not know what I may appear to the world; but to myself I seem to have been only like a boy playing on the seashore, and diverting myself in now and then finding a smoother pebble or a prettier shell than ordinary, while the great ocean of truth lay all undiscovered before me."

CHAPTER FOURTEEN:

Newton in Today's World

Isaac Newton is generally regarded as the greatest man who ever lived. The French mathematician, Legrange, said, "Newton was the greatest genius that ever existed."

But why was he so great?

First, he showed that there was order in the universe. He removed from the minds of people the alarming fears of superstition and magic.

He discovered how gravity holds the universe together. Because of Newton's three laws of motion, scientists can accurately calculate the path of a rocket to the moon.

After the Apollo moon ship blasted away from the earth toward the moon, Mission Control in Houston asked, "Who is doing the driving?"

"Isaac Newton," the astronauts replied promptly.

In book three of *Principia*, Isaac Newton showed by a diagram how a huge cannon on top of a mountain above the atmosphere could be used to fire a man-made satellite into orbit about the earth.

He studied light and color with a prism and wrote *Opticks* one of the most important books about light. He invented the reflecting telescope. The longest telescope in the world (a sun telescope at Kitt Peak National Observatory in Arizona), and the largest telescope in the world (the Mount Palomar telescope in California) are both reflecting telescopes.

Isaac Newton invented fluxions (called *calculus* today). This is a method of mathematics which makes difficult problems easy to solve.

As long as science is studied, Sir Isaac Newton will be remembered.

But there is still much to learn about Isaac's researches into the Bible. When he died, he left more than a million words of notes on the Bible (more than thirty books the size of this one). Even today some of the notes have not been read, much less studied. Not only was Isaac a great scientist, but he was a great Christian and Bible scholar. Yet, this second side of his character is only today, three hundred years later, becoming known to the public.

INDEX

Bibliography

Asimov, Isaac. *Asimov's Biographical Encyclopedia of Science and Technology.* (Garden City: Doubleday & Company, Inc., 1964).

Andrade, Edward Neville Da Costa. *Sir Isaac Newton: Science Study Stories.* (Doubleday Anchor, 1954).

Bixby, William. *The Universe of Galileo and Newton.* (Horizon Periodical, Horizon Caravel, 1964).

Houston, W. Robert and M. Vere DeVault. *Sir Isaac Newton: Scientist-Mathematician.* (Austin: The Steck Company, 1960).

Knight, David C. *Isaac Newton: Mastermind of Modern Science: A First Biography.* (Watts, 1961).

Lerner, Aaron Bunsen. *Einstein and Newton; A Comparison of the Two Greatest Scientists.* (Lerner Publications Company, 1973).

Manuel, Frank E. *A Portrait of Isaac Newton.* (Cambridge: The Belknap Press of Harvard University Press, 1968).

Manuel, Frank E. *Isaac Newton, Historian.* (Cambridge: The Belknap Press of Harvard University Press, 1963).

Moore, Patrick A. *Isaac Newton; Lives to Remember.* (Putnam, 1958).

More, Louis T. *Isaac Newton.* (New York: Charles Scribner's Sons, 1934).

Newton, Isaac. *Mathematical Principles of Natural Philosophy.* (Encyclopaedia Britannica, Inc., 1952).

North, John David. *Isaac Newton.* (Clarendon Biographies, Oxford University Press, 1967).

Schultz, Pearl and Harry. *Isaac Newton; Scientific Genius*. (Champaign, Illinois: Garrard Publishing Company, 1972).

Sootin, Harry. *Isaac Newton*. (Julian Messner, 1955).

Sullivan, J. W. N. *Isaac Newton*. (New York: The Macmillan Co., 1938).

Tannenbaum, Beulah and Myra Stillmann. *Isaac Newton: Pioneer of Space Mathematics*. (New York: Whittlesey House, McGraw-Hill Book Company, 1958).

Thayer, H. S., Editor. *Newton's Philosophy of Nature: Selections from his writings*. (New York: Hafner Press, A Division of Macmillan Publishing Co., Inc., 1953).

Uden, Grant. *They Looked Like This*. (Alden Press; Basil, Blackwell and Matt Ltd., 1965).

SOWERS SERIES

ATHLETE
   Billy Sunday, Home Run to Heaven
     by Robert Allen

EXPLORERS AND PIONEERS
   Christopher Columbus, Adventurer of Faith and Courage
     by Bennie Rhodes
   Johnny Appleseed, God's Faithful Planter, John Chapman
     by David Collins

HOMEMAKERS
   Abigail Adams, First Lady of Faith and Courage
     by Evelyn Witter
   Susanna Wesley, Mother of John and Charles
     by Charles Ludwig

HUMANITARIANS
   Florence Nightingale, God's Servant at the Battlefield
     by David Collins
   Teresa of Calcutta, Serving the Poorest of the Poor
     by D. Jeanene Watson

MUSICIANS AND POETS
   Francis Scott Key, God's Courageous Composer
     by David Collins
   Samuel Francis Smith, My Country, 'Tis of Thee
     by Marguerite E. Fitch